WASHINGTON BUCKET LIST

Set Off on **150 Epic Adventures** and Discover
Incredible Destinations to Live Out Your Dreams
While Creating Unforgettable Memories
that Will Last a Lifetime.

**(Online Digital MAP included - access it through
the link provided in the MAP Chapter of this book)**

BeCrePress Travel

WASHINGTON BUCKET LIST

TABLE OF CONTENTS

WASHINGTON BUCKET LIST

WASHINGTON BUCKET LIST

WASHINGTON BUCKET LIST

WASHINGTON BUCKET LIST

INTRODUCTION

Are you ready to embark on an exciting tour through Washington State? Buckle up, because "Washington Bucket List: Set Off on 150 Epic Adventures" is about to take you on an exciting journey through the state's various landscapes, dynamic cities, and cultural hotspots. This isn't your ordinary travel guide; it's your ultimate companion to the best of what Washington has to offer, offering a trip as lasting as the state's breathtaking mountains and as colorful as its bustling downtown streets.

We've chosen 150 of Washington's most breathtaking sites in this comprehensive guide, each one a hidden gem just waiting to be discovered. This book is your passport to the best of Washington, from the towering peaks of Mount St. Helens and the tranquil waters of Lake Chelan to the bustling streets of Seattle and the serene splendor of the Hoh Rainforest. There's something in here for everyone, whether you're an adrenaline addict, a history buff, a nature lover, or a city slicker.

But we're not simply providing you with a list of places to see. We've created a full guide for each site, replete with descriptions, addresses, nearest cities, driving directions, GPS coordinates, the best times to visit, fees, and even a few amusing facts to stimulate your interest. We've also included the webpage for each destination for your convenience. This is your all-in-one travel guide to Washington, designed to make your trip as easy and pleasurable as possible.

And here's the icing on the cake: we're including an interactive map of Washington state with all of the destinations already recorded as a terrific extra for each reader. This simple digital tool will make exploring all 150 wonderful sites much easier and faster. No more fumbling with paper maps or perplexing navigation apps; with this interactive map, you'll have access to the entire state of Washington.

So, are you ready to embark on a once-in-a-lifetime adventure? You're not just visiting Washington with "Washington Bucket List: Set Off on 150 Epic Adventures", you're experiencing it. You're becoming immersed in its scenery, culture, history, and people. You're not just making a trip; you're making memories. So, what are you holding out for? Your tour across Washington's wonders begins right here. It's only a page away from adventure.

About Washington

To access the Digital Map, please refer to the 'Map Chapter' in this book

Landscape of Washington

By drawing on the rich tapestry of the state's topographical characteristics, we can paint a vibrant picture of Washington's landscape. Washington is located in the contiguous United States' northwesternmost corner, bordering Idaho to the east and Oregon to the south. The Pacific Ocean constitutes its western border, while British Columbia, Canada, forms its northern border.

The state's geography is a study of contrasts. The Cascade line, a large mountain line that runs north-south through the state, divides it in two. Western Washington has a Mediterranean climate, with warm winters, autumns, and springs and relatively dry summers west of the Cascades. Among the active volcanoes in this region are Mount Baker, Glacier Peak, Mount Rainier, Mount St. Helens, and Mount

Adams, with Mount Rainier standing as the state's tallest mountain and a conspicuous feature seen from Seattle.

Western Washington also includes the Olympic Mountains, which are located far west on the Olympic Peninsula. These mountains are home to dense conifer forests and temperate rainforests, notably the Hoh Rainforest, the continental United States only rainforest. Despite having few total inches of rain per year, Western Washington has more rainy days than most other parts of the country.

The terrain in eastern Washington, on the other side of the Cascades, is drastically different. With extensive areas of semiarid steppe and a few really arid deserts in the rain shadow of the Cascades, this region has a somewhat dry climate. Despite the limited rainfall, agriculture thrives in this region due to the extremely fertile soil and extensive irrigation provided by dams along the Columbia River.

The northeastern region of the state is dominated by the Okanogan Highlands, as well as the steep Kettle River Range and Selkirk Mountains. The Palouse region in the southeast was once grassland, but it has since been converted to cultivation and stretches all the way to the Blue Mountains.

In summary, the Washington's topography is diverse, with mountains, forests, farmlands, and dry regions, as well as a range of landscapes and temperatures. Because of its diversity, it is an exciting state to visit, with each region having its own particular charm and character.

Flora and Fauna of Washington

Washington State is a biodiversity hotspot, brimming with a rich array of plant and animal species that represent its different habitats. These ecosystems encompass marine, freshwater, and terrestrial areas, each housing distinct groups of life, making the state a real nature lover's paradise.

The state's forests, which are among the largest in the country, envelop over half of the state's geographical area in a lush embrace. With towering Douglas firs, hemlocks, western red cedars, and ponderosa pines largely occupying the mountain regions, these forests are a tribute to the state's rich botanical past. These tree types not only add to the state's lush foliage, but they also play an important role in its ecosystems, providing a home for a variety of wildlife species.

The semiarid parts of the Columbia basin, in stark contrast to the forested landscapes, showcase a different aspect of the state's vegetation. Grass reigns supreme here, covering the area in a sea of green. The grasslands gradually give way to sagebrush and other scattered bushes as one travels into the driest parts, demonstrating nature's perseverance in less favorable settings.

Washington State's fauna is as diversified as its vegetation. Large creatures found in the state include graceful deer, majestic elk, elusive bears, agile mountain goats, and secretive pumas, also known as cougars. The state also has various fur-bearing species, which adds to its diverse biodiversity.

The Pacific flyway, a key migration route for waterfowl in North America, follows the Puget Sound Lowland. This region, which is peppered with multiple national wildlife refuges, provides sanctuary to a variety of shorebird and marine mammal populations, making it a popular destination for birdwatchers and wildlife enthusiasts.

The state's water bodies are teeming with freshwater game species like trout, bass, grayling, and sturgeon. In addition to this aquatic diversity, five species of Pacific salmon make their epic voyage up the streams of western Washington to spawn, attracting nature lovers from all around.

The coastal bays and Puget Sound provide habitat for a wide range of shellfish, contributing to the state's diverse marine biodiversity. The waters of the San Juan Islands in northwestern Washington, which are part of the upper Puget Sound, are a whale-watcher's paradise. The majestic killer whales, beautiful gray whales, and acrobatic humpback whales are among them.

In conclusion, Washington State's flora and wildlife offer a dynamic picture of biodiversity. From its lush woods and semiarid grasslands to its freshwater and marine environments, the state is home to a diverse array of species. This biodiversity not only enhances the state's natural attractiveness but also plays an important role in maintaining the state's ecological equilibrium. As a result, Washington State is a fascinating location for individuals who want to immerse themselves in the magnificence of nature.

Climate of Washington

Washington State's climate, a significant role in generating its different landscapes and ecosystems, is divided into two parts, each having its own distinct qualities and charm. The state's climatic variability is mostly due to natural characteristics, with the Cascade Range playing a key role in separating two separate climatic zones.

The climate in the western area of Washington State is primarily Mediterranean, with pleasant temperatures throughout the year. Winters, autumns, and springs are often wet in this region, while summers are quite dry, providing a welcome contrast. This region also contains the Cascade Range, which contains active volcanoes such as Mount Baker, Glacier Peak, Mount Rainier, Mount St. Helens, and Mount Adams. Mount Rainier is the tallest and most dangerous of these, due to its closeness to the densely populated Seattle metropolitan region. The Olympic Mountains, which are covered in dense coniferous forests and patches of temperate rainforest, are also found in the western region. Because they are among the only rainforests in the continental United States, these rainforests, such as the Hoh Rainforest, are one-of-a-kind and priceless natural assets.

Eastern Washington, on the other hand, is distinguished by vast swaths of semiarid steppe and a few really arid deserts located in the rain shadow of the Cascades. Despite a lack of rain, the region thrives agriculturally thanks to its good soil and vast irrigation, made possible by dams along the Columbia River. The environment gradually gets less arid as one proceeds east, with yearly rainfall increasing. The Okanogan Highlands, as well as the mountainous landscapes of the Kettle River Range and the Selkirk Mountains, cover the state's northeastern quadrant. The Palouse region, which stretches all the way to the Blue Mountains, was formerly a grassland that has been mostly turned into profitable farming.

The interaction of the massive semi-permanent low-pressure and high-pressure systems of the north Pacific Ocean, North American continental air masses, and the Olympic and Cascade mountains affects Washington's overall climate. The prevailing winds from the northwest deliver relatively cool air and a predictable dry season during the spring and summer. In the autumn and winter, however, the winds turn to the southwest, bringing cooler, cloudy weather and a reliably wet season. The phrase "Pineapple Express" refers to atmospheric river events in which numerous storm systems are directed by a persistent cyclone from the tropical Pacific areas a long distance into the Pacific Northwest, resulting in substantial rainfall. This climatic phenomenon adds to Washington State's climatic diversity and richness.

History of Washington

Washington state, nestled in the heart of the Pacific Northwest, is a historical tapestry rich with tales of ancient civilizations, daring explorers, territorial struggles, and the birth of a modern industrial powerhouse. This chapter transports you back in time, following the steps of the state's initial residents, European explorers, early settlers, and visionaries who determined the state's fate.

Washington's story begins thousands of years ago when the region served as a cradle for ancient civilizations. Indigenous tribes prospered amidst the region's different settings, from coastal tribes gathering the bounty of the sea to Plateau tribes cultivating the fertile soils, providing the groundwork for Washington's rich cultural legacy.

With the entrance of European explorers in the late 18th century, a new age began. Expeditions made by Spanish explorer Juan Pérez and British Captain James Cook mapped the region's rough shores, paving the way for further exploration and settlement.

In the nineteenth century, the promise of the West drew a flood of American settlers. Many traveled the Oregon Trail, with some traveling north into the Puget Sound area, heralding the beginning of American colonies in the region. Concurrently, the British built Fort Nisqually, laying the groundwork for future territorial negotiations.

Washington proudly became the 42nd state of the United States after emerging from the shadow of the Oregon Territory in 1889. The state's early economy was a patchwork of agriculture, lumber, and mining, reflecting the state's natural resources.

Washington was at the vanguard of progressive principles at the beginning of the twentieth century, with the women's club movement empowering women with leadership possibilities and political influence, altering the state's political landscape.

Even throughout the Great Depression's economic troubles, Washington displayed endurance and innovation. During a time of national struggle, the development of electrical dams along the Columbia River, culminating in the majestic Grand Coulee Dam, represented optimism and progress.

World War II transformed Washington into a hub for the war industry, with corporations like Boeing leading the drive and ports around the state providing a regular stream of ships to the war effort.

When Mount St. Helens erupted in 1980, changing the landscape and leaving an indelible impact on Washington's history, the latter half of the twentieth century witnessed a stunning demonstration of nature's power.

Today, Washington is a beacon of innovation and entrepreneurship, with global behemoths such as Microsoft, Amazon.com, Boeing, and Starbucks attesting to the state's lasting spirit of innovation and entrepreneurship.

Since the mid-twentieth century, Washington has leaned Democratic, with its unique system of blanket primaries, which let voters choose any candidate regardless of party affiliation, being a hallmark of its progressive principles until it was found unlawful in 2003.

Remember that every mountain, river, and city in Washington state has a tale to tell. Washington's history is as rich and vibrant as its surroundings, ranging from ancient indigenous societies to modern tech titans. This rich tapestry of history sets the setting for the adventures that await you in the next chapters.

AMBOY

Mount St. Helens National Volcanic Monument

Immerse yourself in the raw power of nature at Mount St. Helens National Volcanic Monument. This massive stratovolcano located in Skamania County, Washington, erupted in 1980, devastating the surrounding area but leaving behind a stark beauty that continues to fascinate visitors.

Location: 42218 NE Yale Bridge Rd, Amboy, WA 98601-4601

Closest City or Town: Amboy, Washington

How to Get There: From Amboy, take the NE Yale Bridge Rd and follow the signs to the monument.

GPS Coordinates: 45.927549° N, 122.3812118° W

Best Time to Visit: Late spring through early fall.

Pass/Permit/Fees: $8 per person.

Did You Know? The 1980 eruption of Mount St. Helens is considered the most disastrous volcanic eruption in the history of the United States.

Website: http://www.fs.fed.us/gpnf/mshnvm/

ANACORTES

Washington Park

Immerse yourself in the lush greenery and breathtaking vistas of Washington Park. Located on the shores of Anacortes, Fidalgo Island, Washington Park offers visitors an unparalleled experience of the Pacific Northwest's beauty. Enjoy a variety of activities such as camping, picnicking, hiking, or simply soaking in the stunning ocean views. The park's unique feature is its Loop Road, a scenic 2.2-mile drive that offers panoramic views of the surrounding landscape.

Location: Sunset Avenue, Anacortes, Fidalgo Island, WA 98221

Closest City or Town: Anacortes, Washington

How to Get There: From Anacortes, take Commercial Avenue and turn west onto 12th Street. Continue on this street as it becomes Sunset Avenue and leads straight to Washington Park.

GPS Coordinates: 48.4948° N, 122.6758° W

Best Time to Visit: The park is open year-round, with the peak season being the summer months for camping.

Pass/Permit/Fees: The park is free for day use. Overnight camping fees apply.

Did You Know? Washington Park sits on a peninsula at the western edge of Fidalgo Island, offering beautiful vistas of the ocean and the surrounding islands.

Website:
http://www.cityofanacortes.org/parks/WaPark/wa_park.htm

Mt Erie Park

Revel in the tranquility of nature at Mt Erie Park, a hidden gem located in Anacortes, on Fidalgo Island, Washington. With panoramic views of the surrounding landscape, it's a paradise for photographers and nature enthusiasts alike. Hike through the lush trails, relish a peaceful picnic, or challenge yourself with rock climbing. The pinnacle of the park is its namesake, Mt Erie, which stands as the highest point on Fidalgo Island.

Location: Ray Auld Drive and Heart Lake Road, Anacortes, Fidalgo Island, WA 98221

Closest City or Town: Anacortes, Washington

How to Get There: From Anacortes, take WA-20 E and turn onto Campbell Lake Rd. Follow signs for Mt Erie Park.

GPS Coordinates: 48.4689249° N, 122.6294605° W

Best Time to Visit: Spring and Summer are the perfect seasons to visit.

Pass/Permit/Fees: The park is free to visit.

Did You Know? Mt Erie is named after Erie, Pennsylvania, the original home of Amos Bowman, the founder of Anacortes.

Website: http://www.cityofanacortes.org/parks/parks.htm

Cap Sante Park

Discover a hidden gem in the Pacific Northwest at Cap Sante Park, an ideal spot for those seeking tranquillity amidst nature. Overlooking Anacortes, Washington, the park captivates visitors with panoramic views of the city, marina, and the surrounding islands. From hiking trails to picnic spots, it's a haven for outdoor enthusiasts. The park's uniqueness lies in its stunning viewpoints, making it an irresistible draw for photographers and nature lovers alike.

Location: 807 W Ave, Anacortes, WA 98221

Closest City or Town: Anacortes, Washington

How to Get There: From the city center of Anacortes, head east on 12th Street until you reach W Avenue. Follow W Avenue north until you reach the park.

GPS Coordinates: 48.513283° N, 122.6022476° W

Best Time to Visit: It is open year-round, but the spring and summer months offer the most pleasant weather.

Pass/Permit/Fees: No entrance fees are required.

Did You Know? Despite its peaceful atmosphere today, Cap Sante was originally a bustling logging site in the late 19th century.

WASHINGTON BUCKET LIST

Website: http://members.anacortes.org/list/member/cap-sante-park-1278

ASHFORD

Mount Rainier National Park

Unleash your inner explorer at Mount Rainier National Park, a paradise for nature lovers. Nestled in the heart of Washington, the park offers a range of activities from hiking to stargazing, with the majestic Mount Rainier serving as a stunning backdrop. Don't miss the chance to capture the picturesque sunrise at the park's highest point!

Location: V7HF+X6 Sunrise, Washington

Closest City or Town: Seattle, Washington

How to Get There: Take the WA-7 S from Tacoma, then switch to WA-706 E to reach the park.

GPS Coordinates: 46.8799375° N, 121.7269375° W

Best Time to Visit: Summer months (June to September) for the best weather and access to all hiking trails.

Pass/Permit/Fees: Fees vary depending on the type of access (car, foot, etc.). Check their website for the most recent information.

Did You Know? Mount Rainier is an active stratovolcano, the most heavily glaciated peak in the lower 48 states!

Website: http://www.nps.gov/mora/index.htm

BAINBRIDGE ISLAND

Bloedel Reserve

Experience the beauty of nature at Bloedel Reserve, a stunning 150-acre garden located on Bainbridge Island in Washington. Nestled among towering trees and lush gardens, this destination offers visitors the opportunity to explore the wonders of nature.

Location: 7571 NE Dolphin Dr, Bainbridge Island, WA 98110-3001

Closest City or Town: Bainbridge Island, Washington

How to Get There: Take SR-305 N from downtown Bainbridge Island and drive until you reach Bloedel Reserve.

GPS Coordinates: 47.7080312° N, 122.5475964° W

Best Time to Visit: Spring is the perfect time to explore Bloedel Reserve, as the gardens are in full bloom and the days are mild.

Pass/Permit/Fees: Admission fees apply.

Did You Know? Bloedel Reserve is home to over 20 different species of birds!

Website: http://www.bloedelreserve.org/

Bainbridge Island Museum of Art

Discover a collection of thought-provoking and diverse artworks at the Bainbridge Island Museum of Art. Nestled in the heart of Bainbridge Island, this contemporary art museum offers rotating exhibits, showcasing the talent of local and regional artists. Don't miss the museum's unique "green" architecture, which is a work of art in itself!

Location: 550 Winslow Way E, Bainbridge Island, WA 98110-2418

Closest City or Town: Seattle, Washington (A short ferry ride away)

How to Get There: From Seattle, take the Seattle-Bainbridge Island ferry. The museum is within walking distance from the ferry terminal.

GPS Coordinates: 47.6251967° N, 122.5145488° W

Best Time to Visit: Open year-round. The museum is indoor, so it can be enjoyed in any weather condition.

Pass/Permit/Fees: Admission is free.

Did You Know? The museum is committed to sustainability and has been designed to meet LEED Gold standards.

Website: http://www.biartmuseum.org/

BELLEVUE

Bellevue Botanical Garden

Unleash your inner botanist at the Bellevue Botanical Garden, spanning 53 acres of cultivated gardens, woodlands, and wetlands. The garden is renowned for its exquisitely maintained landscapes featuring a diverse collection of plants, offering a tranquil retreat for nature lovers.

Location: 12001 Main St, Bellevue, WA 98005-3522

Closest City or Town: Bellevue, Washington

How to Get There: From Bellevue, take NE 8th St to Main St. Follow Main St to the garden.

GPS Coordinates: 47.6091817° N, 122.179617° W

Best Time to Visit: Year-round, with different sections of the garden coming to life in different seasons.

Pass/Permit/Fees: Free. No passes or fees are required.

Did You Know? The Bellevue Botanical Garden hosts a stunning Garden d'Lights event every winter, transforming the garden into a blossoming winter wonderland.

Website: http://www.bellevuebotanical.org/

Downtown Park

Unwind in the heart of Bellevue at Downtown Park, an urban oasis perfect for picnics, walks, or just taking in the sights. This 20-acre park, often described as the "Central Park" of Bellevue, offers a beautiful half-mile promenade surrounded by a double row of shade trees, a large water canal, and a stunning 240-foot wide waterfall.

Location: 10201 Northeast Fourth St, Bellevue, WA 98005

Closest City or Town: Bellevue, Washington

How to Get There: From I-405, take NE 4th St exit (exit 13A) and head west for about half a mile. Downtown Park will be on your right.

GPS Coordinates: 47.6129089° N, 122.2041805° W

Best Time to Visit: Year-round, but summer offers outdoor movies and concerts

Pass/Permit/Fees: The park is free to enter.

Did You Know? Downtown Park was designed by the world-renowned landscape architect, Richard Haag.

Website: http://bellevue.com/attraction.php?id=168

Bellevue Square

Indulge in an upscale shopping experience at Bellevue Square, located in the heart of Bellevue, Washington. This premier shopping center offers a mix of top-notch stores, trendy restaurants, and entertainment venues. The Kid's Cove play area and the regular events are unique features that make Bellevue Square more than just a shopping spot.

Location: 405 Bellevue Square, Bellevue, WA 98004, United States

Closest City or Town: Bellevue, Washington

How to Get There: From Bellevue, take NE 8th St to Bellevue Way NE. Turn right onto Bellevue Way NE, and you will find Bellevue Square on your right.

GPS Coordinates: 47.614205° N, 122.2028976° W

Best Time to Visit: Open year-round, but the holiday season is an especially festive time to visit.

Pass/Permit/Fees: No entrance fees. Parking is free.

Did You Know? Bellevue Square is part of the Bellevue Collection, which also includes Bellevue Place and Lincoln Square.

Website: http://bellevuecollection.com/

BELLINGHAM

Whatcom Falls Park

Immerse yourself in the lush green world of Whatcom Falls Park, a tranquil oasis tucked away in Bellingham, Washington. Amble along the winding trails, breathe in the crisp air and be charmed by the park's centerpiece - a magnificent waterfall cascading over stone bridges.

Location: 1401 Electric Ave, Bellingham, WA 98229-2435

Closest City or Town: Bellingham, Washington

How to Get There: From downtown Bellingham, head east on W Holly St and continue on Lakeway Dr. Turn right on Electric Ave and follow it straight to the park.

GPS Coordinates: 48.7504475° N, 122.4269053° W

Best Time to Visit: Spring to early fall for the best weather and fullest water flow.

Pass/Permit/Fees: Entrance is free.

Did You Know? The park has four sets of waterfalls and the old stone bridge crossing is a popular spot for photographs.

Website: http://www.cob.org/services/recreation/parks-trails/Pages/whatcom-falls-park.aspx

Fairhaven Historic District

Step back in time as you explore the Fairhaven Historic District, a charming enclave filled with 19th-century architecture, cobblestone streets, and quaint boutiques. Located in Bellingham's south side, this district is brimming with history and character.

Location: 1100 Harris Ave, Bellingham, WA 98225-7037

Closest City or Town: Bellingham, Washington

How to Get There: From I-5, take exit 250 and head west on Old Fairhaven Pkwy. Turn right onto 12th St and follow it straight to Fairhaven.

GPS Coordinates: 48.7199249° N, 122.5031463° W

Best Time to Visit: Year-round, but the summer months offer a wealth of outdoor activities and festivals.

Pass/Permit/Fees: The district is free to explore, but individual attractions may have fees.

Did You Know? Fairhaven was once a separate city before merging with Bellingham in 1903.

Website: http://www.fairhaven.com/

Chuckanut Drive

Drive through the mesmerizing coastal road of Chuckanut Drive, a 24-mile-long scenic drive situated just south of Bellingham, WA. With the breathtaking views of the San Juan Islands and the Cascade Mountains, this drive offers amazing sights at every turn, making it the perfect road trip for any nature lover.

Location: 100-104 WA-11, Bellingham, WA 98229

Closest City or Town: Bellingham, Washington

How to Get There: From Bellingham, go south on I-5 and take exit 250 for WA-11 S/Chuckanut Drive.

GPS Coordinates: 48.6481402° N, 122.4868998° W

Best Time to Visit: Anytime, although summers and fall tend to offer the best weather and scenery.

Pass/Permit/Fees: Free of charge.

Did You Know? Chuckanut Drive is the only location in Washington where the Cascade mountains meet the sea.

Website: https://www.scenicwa.com/chuckanut-drive

Boulevard Park

Welcome to Boulevard Park, a charming urban oasis nestled along the shores of Bellingham Bay. This park, located on Bayview Drive in Bellingham, offers scenic walking trails, an over-water boardwalk, and a great playground for kids. Don't miss the unique opportunity to watch the stunning sunset over the bay, making it an iconic location in the city.

Location: 470 Bayview Dr, Bellingham, WA 98225-7804

Closest City or Town: Bellingham, Washington

How to Get There: From Bellingham, head west on Bayview Drive. The park is located on the right.

GPS Coordinates: 48.7312585° N, 122.5030982° W

Best Time to Visit: Open year-round, but particularly beautiful in summer and fall.

Pass/Permit/Fees: Free entrance.

Did You Know? Boulevard Park is one of the most photographed locations in the city due to its stunning sunset views.

Website: http://www.cob.org/services/recreation/parks-trails/Pages/boulevard-park.aspx

Lake Padden Park

Discover the serene beauty of Lake Padden Park, a tranquil locale nestled amidst the hills of south Bellingham. At Lake Padden, visitors can engage in a multitude of outdoor activities such as hiking, swimming, fishing, and picnicking. The lake's unique feature is the beautiful 2.6-mile trail that encircles it, offering stunning views of nature's beauty.

Location: 4882 South Samish Way, Bellingham, WA 98229-3444

Closest City or Town: Bellingham, Washington

How to Get There: From Bellingham, head south on Samish Way. Turn left at the sign for Lake Padden Park.

GPS Coordinates: 48.6981313° N, 122.4421247° W

Best Time to Visit: Open year-round, but spring to fall is the best time to enjoy outdoor activities.

Pass/Permit/Fees: Free entrance.

Did You Know? Lake Padden is named after Michael Padden, the man who homesteaded the area in the 19th century.

Website: http://www.cob.org/services/recreation/parks-trails/lake-padden-park.aspx

BLAINE

Peace Arch State Park

Experience the tranquility of Peace Arch State Park, nestled in the quiet town of Blaine, Washington. This unique park straddles the US-Canada border and is home to the iconic Peace Arch monument. Enjoy leisurely walks around the park, marvel at the beautiful gardens, or picnic while soaking in the stunning views of the surrounding mountains.

Location: 19 A St, Blaine, WA 98230

Closest City or Town: Blaine, Washington

How to Get There: From Blaine, head west on 2nd St towards Peace Portal Dr, then turn right onto Peace Portal Dr and left onto A St.

GPS Coordinates: 49.0017062° N, 122.7554463° W

Best Time to Visit: Open year-round, but spring is particularly beautiful when the gardens are in bloom.

Pass/Permit/Fees: Entry is free.

Did You Know? The Peace Arch monument was built to commemorate the centennial of the Treaty of Ghent, which ended the War of 1812.

Website: https://parks.state.wa.us/562/Peace-Arch

BREMERTON

USS Turner Joy Museum Ship

Embark on a journey through maritime history at the USS Turner Joy Museum Ship, docked in Bremerton, Washington. This legendary Navy destroyer participated in the Vietnam War and now serves as an interactive museum. Discover the ship's brave past, explore its many compartments, and learn about the lives of the sailors who once called it home.

Location: 300 Washington Beach Ave, Bremerton, WA 98337-5668

Closest City or Town: Bremerton, Washington

How to Get There: From Seattle, take the Seattle-Bremerton ferry. The museum is a short walk from the Bremerton Ferry Terminal.

GPS Coordinates: 47.5646113° N, 122.6228315° W

Best Time to Visit: Open year-round, with summer being the most popular time to visit.

Pass/Permit/Fees: Admission is $14 for adults, $9 for children. Discounts are available for seniors and the military.

Did You Know? The USS Turner Joy was one of the last Forrest Sherman-class destroyers built for the US Navy.

Website: http://www.ussturnerjoy.org/info.html

Puget Sound Navy Museum

Delve deep into the rich naval history of the Pacific Northwest at the Puget Sound Navy Museum. Located in Bremerton, Washington, the museum is home to a vast array of exhibits showcasing the Navy's influence on the region. With interactive displays and a wealth of naval artifacts, it's a must-visit for history buffs. The museum's unique feature is an exhibit on the special relationship between the U.S. Navy and the people of Puget Sound.

Location: 251 1st St, Bremerton, WA 98337-5612

Closest City or Town: Bremerton, Washington

How to Get There: From downtown Bremerton, head north on Washington Avenue until you reach 1st Street. The museum is on the corner of 1st Street and Washington Avenue.

GPS Coordinates: 47.5630845° N, 122.6265228° W

Best Time to Visit: The museum is open all year, although it is closed on some federal holidays.

Pass/Permit/Fees: Admission to the museum is free.

Did You Know? The museum is located within a historic building that was once the city's post office.

Website: http://www.pugetsoundnavymuseum.org/

CASTLE ROCK

Mount St. Helens Visitor Center

Experience the incredible power of nature at Mount St. Helens Visitor Center, located a mere five miles from Castle Rock, Washington. Here you can learn about the enormous eruption of 1980 that reshaped the landscape, and take in stunning views of the once-again tranquil volcano. Participate in educational programs and explore exhibit halls housing geologic and botanical displays.

Location: Hwy. 504, milepost 5, Castle Rock, WA 98611

Closest City or Town: Castle Rock, Washington

How to Get There: From Castle Rock, follow Hwy 504 eastward for approximately 5 miles. The visitor center will be on your left.

GPS Coordinates: 46.2868033° N, 122.8996692° W

Best Time to Visit: Open year-round, but eruption anniversary events in May offer a unique experience.

Pass/Permit/Fees: Entry fees apply, please check the website for the latest pricing.

Did You Know? The visitor center was among the first facilities to open to the public after the 1980 eruption.

Website: http://parks.state.wa.us/245/Mount-St-Helens

CHELAN

Lady of the Lake

Unveil the beauty of Lake Chelan on the Lady of the Lake, a renowned passenger ferry service in Washington. Nestled at 1418 W Woodin Ave, Chelan, this ferry offers you the opportunity to witness the breathtaking cascades and crystal-clear waters of Lake Chelan. All aboard for an unforgettable tour brimming with scenic vistas and unique wildlife spotting!

Location: 1418 W Woodin Ave, Chelan, WA 98816-9150

Closest City or Town: Chelan, Washington

How to Get There: Head north on WA-150 E/ E Woodin Ave toward N Emerson St, then make a left turn onto N Sanders St. Turn right at the second cross street onto W Woodin Ave.

GPS Coordinates: 47.83606° N, 120.0380622° W

Best Time to Visit: Summer months, when the lake is calm and clear.

Pass/Permit/Fees: Prices vary based on tour type and duration. Visit the website for more information.

Did You Know? The Lady of the Lake provides the only ferry services to Stehekin and the North Cascades National Park.

Website: http://www.ladyofthelake.com/

Lake Chelan

Plunge into the crystal-clear waters of Lake Chelan, a beautiful freshwater lake nestled in the North Cascades of Washington. Offering a unique combination of spectacular scenery and plentiful recreational activities, Lake Chelan is a paradise for water enthusiasts and nature lovers alike. Dive in and experience the tranquility and beauty of this one-of-a-kind destination.

Location: Lake Chelan Marina, Chelan, WA 98816

Closest City or Town: Chelan, Washington

How to Get There: From Chelan, follow the signs to Lake Chelan State Park.

GPS Coordinates: 47.8408323° N, 120.0168079° W

Best Time to Visit: Summer for water activities.

Pass/Permit/Fees: Free access, but fees may apply for certain activities.

Did You Know? At 50.5 miles long, Lake Chelan is the third deepest lake in the United States.

Website: http://www.tildio.com/

Slidewaters

Get ready for a day full of splashes and fun at Slidewaters in Chelan, Washington. This family-friendly waterpark is home to a variety of exciting water slides, a lazy river, and a kid's aqua zoo. It's the ideal place to escape the summer heat!

Location: 102 Waterslide Dr, Chelan, WA 98816

Closest City or Town: Chelan, Washington

How to Get There: From Chelan, take Manson Hwy and turn on Waterslide Dr. The park will be on your right.

GPS Coordinates: 47.8339758° N, 120.0352655° W

Best Time to Visit: Summer months of June through August when temperatures are warm.

Pass/Permit/Fees: Admission fee required, varies based on age and height.

Did You Know? Slidewaters is home to the largest water slide in Washington state!

Website: http://www.slidewaters.com/

COULEE DAM

Grand Coulee Dam

Experience the sheer power and grandeur of the Grand Coulee Dam, one of the largest concrete structures in the world. Located on the Columbia River in Washington, this engineering marvel offers exciting tours and a mesmerizing nightly laser light show during the summer!

Location: Grand Coulee Dam, Visitors Access Route, Coulee Dam, WA 99116, United States

Closest City or Town: Coulee Dam, Washington

How to Get There: From Spokane, WA, take US-2 W and US-395 N to WA-155 N in Coulee Dam.

GPS Coordinates: 47.9565529° N, 118.9809849° W

Best Time to Visit: Spring through fall for the best weather and to see the laser light show.

Pass/Permit/Fees: Free entry and tours.

Did You Know? Grand Coulee Dam is one of the world's largest producers of hydroelectric power.

Website: http://www.usbr.gov/pn/grandcoulee/

COUPEVILLE

Fort Casey State Park

Immerse yourself in history at Fort Casey State Park. Located on Whidbey Island in Washington, the park is home to a historic fort that functioned as a defense installation during both World Wars. Enjoy a stroll around the park's trails, or discover the wonders of marine life at the tide pools.

Location: 1280 Engle Rd, Coupeville, WA 98239

Closest City or Town: Seattle, Washington

How to Get There: From Seattle, take the WA-20 W and then WA-525 N to reach the park.

GPS Coordinates: 48.1608372° N, 122.6810493° W

Best Time to Visit: Anytime from spring to fall.

Pass/Permit/Fees: A Discover Pass is required for vehicle access to state parks for day use. The current fee is $30 annually or $10 for a day pass.

Did You Know? Fort Casey, along with Fort Worden and Fort Flagler, once formed a "Triangle of Fire" to protect the entrance to Puget Sound.

Website:
http://www.parks.wa.gov/parkpage.asp?selectedpark=Fort%20Casey

Ebey's Landing National Historical Reserve

Explore the preserved rural landscapes of Ebey's Landing National Historical Reserve in Coupeville, Washington. Here, you can walk through historic farms, visit 19th-century houses, and hike along the scenic bluff trail overlooking Puget Sound and the Olympic Mountains. The reserve offers a unique glimpse into the past, preserving the heart of Ebey's Island.

Location: Parking lot, Ebey's Landing Rd, Coupeville, WA 98239

Closest City or Town: Coupeville, Washington

How to Get There: From Coupeville, take S Main St and turn onto Ebey's Landing Rd. Follow the road until you reach the parking lot.

GPS Coordinates: 48.1924303° N, 122.7085304° W

Best Time to Visit: The reserve is beautiful year-round, but spring and fall offer exceptional weather and fewer crowds.

Pass/Permit/Fees: Entry to the reserve is free.

Did You Know? The reserve is named after Isaac Ebey, the first permanent European-American settler on Whidbey Island.

Website: http://www.nps.gov/ebla/

EASTSOUND

Orcas Island Pottery

Indulge in creativity at Orcas Island Pottery, the oldest pottery studio in the Pacific Northwest. Located in Eastsound, Orcas Island, the studio offers hands-on pottery classes amidst the beauty of nature. Here, even beginners can mold their own masterpieces under expert guidance.

Location: 338 Old Pottery Rd, Eastsound, Orcas Island, WA 98245-9319

Closest City or Town: Eastsound, Washington

How to Get There: From Eastsound, head southeast on Main St toward N Beach Rd. Turn right onto Old Pottery Rd and the destination will be on the right.

GPS Coordinates: 48.6832729° N, 122.9618078° W

Best Time to Visit: Open year-round, but check the website for specific class schedules.

Pass/Permit/Fees: Prices vary depending on the class. Visit the website for more details.

Did You Know? Orcas Island Pottery has been creating unique pieces since 1949!

Website: http://www.orcasislandpottery.com/

EATONVILLE

Northwest Trek Wildlife Park

Dive into the wilderness at Northwest Trek Wildlife Park situated in Eatonville, Washington. Here, you can embark on a tram tour through a 435-acre free-roaming area, home to a myriad of native Northwest animals such as moose, bison, and elk. This is the place for an awe-inspiring encounter with wildlife in their natural surroundings.

Location: 11610 Trek Dr. E, Eatonville, WA 98328-9502

Closest City or Town: Eatonville, Washington

How to Get There: From Eatonville, head east on Center St E. Turn right onto Lynch Creek Rd E. After a mile, take a left onto Trek Dr. E. Follow signs to the park.

GPS Coordinates: 46.9148095° N, 122.2762975° W

Best Time to Visit: Open year-round, but spring and fall migrations offer unique wildlife viewing opportunities.

Pass/Permit/Fees: Fees vary based on age and membership status, check the website for details.

Did You Know? The park's 725 acres are home to over 200 species of native Northwest wildlife.

Website: http://www.nwtrek.org/

EVERETT

Flying Heritage & Combat Armor Museum

Embark on a journey through history at the Flying Heritage & Combat Armor Museum, located in Everett. Discover a vast collection of historically significant aircraft and tanks, perfectly restored to their original condition. This is an experience that promises to be both educational and inspiring.

Location: 3407 109th St SW, Everett, WA 98204-1351

Closest City or Town: Everett, Washington

How to Get There: From Everett, head south on I-5 S. Take exit 186 for WA-96 E. Turn left onto 128th St SW/WA-96 E. Turn right onto 4th Ave W. Turn left onto 112th St SW. Turn right onto 3rd Ave SE. The museum will be on your right.

GPS Coordinates: 47.8994971° N, 122.2799935° W

Best Time to Visit: The museum is open year-round, but special events and demonstrations are often held during the summer months.

Pass/Permit/Fees: Entrance fees apply. Please check the website for details.

Did You Know? The museum's collection was started by Microsoft co-founder Paul Allen!

Website: https://flyingheritage.org/

Imagine Children's Museum

Ignite the spark of creativity and learning at the Imagine Children's Museum. Located at 1502 Wall St, Everett, this interactive museum offers a variety of exhibits and activities that promote learning through play. The museum's unique feature is its rooftop playground, which offers spectacular views of the city.

Location: 1502 Wall St, Everett, WA 98201-4008

Closest City or Town: Everett, Washington

How to Get There: From downtown Everett, head south on Colby Ave towards Wall St. Turn right onto Wall St, and the destination will be on the right.

GPS Coordinates: 47.9775138° N, 122.2096228° W

Best Time to Visit: The museum is open year-round, with extended hours during school holidays.

Pass/Permit/Fees: Admission varies by age. Check the website for current prices.

Did You Know? The museum's rooftop is not just a playground, but also houses a dinosaur-themed garden!

Website: http://www.imaginecm.org/

FRIDAY HARBOR

Lime Kiln Point State Park

Join the watch for majestic orcas at Lime Kiln Point State Park, a prime location for whale watching. Located on the west side of San Juan Island in Washington, this park features a historic lighthouse and mesmerizing views of the Haro Strait.

Location: 1567 Westside Rd, Friday Harbor, San Juan Island, WA 98250-8602

Closest City or Town: Friday Harbor, Washington

How to Get There: From Friday Harbor, head west on Spring St toward 2nd St, then turn right onto Argyle Ave. Continue onto Westside Rd to reach the park.

GPS Coordinates: 48.5158674° N, 123.1509604° W

Best Time to Visit: May through September, when whales are most commonly sighted

Pass/Permit/Fees: State Park pass required

Did You Know? Lime Kiln Point is considered one of the best places in the world to view whales from land!

Website: http://www.parks.wa.gov/

The Whale Museum

Immerse yourself in the awe-inspiring world of marine life at The Whale Museum, nestled in the charming town of Friday Harbor on San Juan Island, Washington. The museum offers an engaging and informative exploration of the region's diverse cetacean species, with interactive exhibits and fascinating displays.

Location: 62 1st St N, Friday Harbor, San Juan Island, WA 98250-8337

Closest City or Town: Friday Harbor, Washington

How to Get There: The museum is right in the heart of Friday Harbor, easily accessible by foot from the ferry dock.

GPS Coordinates: 48.5357715° N, 123.0172312° W

Best Time to Visit: Open all year round, but summer months offer better whale-watching opportunities.

Pass/Permit/Fees: Museum admission required, check the website for current prices.

Did You Know? The Whale Museum is the first museum in the country dedicated to the preservation of whales through education and research.

Website: http://www.whalemuseum.org/

Pelindaba Lavender Farm

Step into a purple paradise at Pelindaba Lavender Farm, located in the Friday Harbor of San Juan Island. Wander through the fragrant fields of lavender, indulge in gourmet lavender food products, and learn about the distillation process in their on-site essential oil distillery.

Location: 45 Hawthorne Ln, Friday Harbor, San Juan Island, WA 98250-5008

Closest City or Town: Friday Harbor, Washington

How to Get There: From Friday Harbor, follow Mullis Street westwards out of town. After about a mile, turn left onto Douglas Road and follow the signs to the farm.

GPS Coordinates: 48.5088672° N, 123.0991113° W

Best Time to Visit: The farm is open year-round, but the lavender blooms from mid-July to August.

Pass/Permit/Fees: Free admission.

Did You Know? Pelindaba Lavender Farm is a premier grower of lavender plants, a distiller of lavender essential oils, and a handcrafter of lavender products.

Website: http://www.pelindabalavender.com/

GOLDENDALE

Maryhill Museum of Art

Residing atop a hill overlooking the Columbia River, the Maryhill Museum of Art is a treasure trove of diverse art and historical artifacts. Housed in a castle-like chateau, this museum is home to an eclectic collection that ranges from Native American art to European paintings and sculptures. The outdoor sculpture garden is a unique feature that further enhances the museum's charm.

Location: 35 Maryhill Museum Dr, Goldendale, WA 98620-4601

Closest City or Town: Goldendale, Washington

How to Get There: From Goldendale, take US-97 S, then turn right onto Maryhill Hwy. Follow the signs to the museum.

GPS Coordinates: 45.6775104° N, 120.8647837° W

Best Time to Visit: Open from March to November, with peak season during the summer months.

Pass/Permit/Fees: General admission fee applies; check their website for details.

Did You Know? The museum building was originally intended as a mansion for Samuel Hill, a businessman, and advocate of good roads, but it was turned into a museum instead!

Website: http://www.maryhillmuseum.org/

Stonehenge Memorial

Experience a slice of ancient history in the heart of Washington at the Stonehenge Memorial! This full-size replica of the original Stonehenge in England is a World War I memorial, constructed by Sam Hill. It's located in Goldendale, offering panoramic views of the Columbia River.

Location: 97 Stonehenge Dr, Goldendale, WA 98620

Closest City or Town: Goldendale, WA

How to Get There: From Goldendale, drive south on U.S. Route 97. Turn right on Stonehenge Drive to reach the monument.

GPS Coordinates: 45.6944872° N, 120.8059186° W

Best Time to Visit: Open year-round. But, the memorial looks spectacular at sunrise or sunset.

Pass/Permit/Fees: Free and open to the public.

Did You Know? This was the first memorial in the USA to honor the military personnel who died in World War I.

Website: http://www.maryhillmuseum.org/visit/stonehenge-memorial

Maryhill Winery

Dive into the world of wines at Maryhill Winery, a renowned vineyard located on Highway 14 in Goldendale. Set within the stunning Columbia River Gorge, the winery offers an array of tastings and tours to take you on a journey through the world of wine production. Paired with breathtaking panoramic views, this experience is not to be missed!

Location: 9774 Highway 14, Goldendale, WA 98620-4648

Closest City or Town: Goldendale, Washington

How to Get There: Head east on WA-14 E from Goldendale. The winery will be on your right.

GPS Coordinates: 45.6722265° N, 120.8816507° W

Best Time to Visit: Summer and Fall are ideal for wine-tasting tours.

Pass/Permit/Fees: Tasting fees may apply, please check the website for details.

Did You Know? Maryhill Winery is one of the largest wineries in Washington, producing over 80 different varietals.

Website: http://www.maryhillwinery.com/

ILWACO

Cape Disappointment State Park

Don't let the name fool you, there's nothing disappointing about Cape Disappointment State Park. Located at the mouth of the Columbia River, this park covers 1,882 acres of diverse scenery, from dense forest to sandy beaches. Visitors can enjoy hiking, fishing, boating, and camping, all while taking in stunning views.

Location: 244 Robert Gray Dr. SW, Ilwaco, WA 98624-9165

Closest City or Town: Ilwaco, Washington

How to Get There: The park is accessible via US-101, just 5 miles southwest of Ilwaco.

GPS Coordinates: 46.2780671° N, 124.0537889° W

Best Time to Visit: Summer for camping and beach activities, winter for storm watching

Pass/Permit/Fees: Discovery Pass required ($10/day or $30/year)

Did You Know? The park is named after Captain John Meares' first thwarted voyage to find the Columbia River.

Website: http://parks.state.wa.us/486/Cape-Disappointment

Cape Disappointment Lighthouse

Prepare for an experience anything but disappointing at Cape Disappointment Lighthouse. Standing tall on the southwest corner of Washington, this historic lighthouse offers breathtaking views of the Pacific Ocean. Take a stroll along the lighthouse trail, indulge in bird-watching, or just enjoy the serene ambiance. The lighthouse itself, an active aid to navigation, is the unique feature of this destination.

Location: Cape Disappointment Lighthouse, Cape Disappointment Trail, Ilwaco, WA 98624

Closest City or Town: Ilwaco, Washington

How to Get There: From Ilwaco, follow signs for Cape Disappointment State Park. Once in the park, follow signs to the lighthouse.

GPS Coordinates: 46.2758298° N, 124.0521426° W

Best Time to Visit: The park is open all year, but the best time to visit is during the summer months when the weather is more predictable.

Pass/Permit/Fees: A Discover Pass is required for vehicle access to the park.

Did You Know? Cape Disappointment got its name from Captain John Meares, who was disappointed when he couldn't find the Columbia River.

Website: http://parks.state.wa.us/

North Head Lighthouse

Step back in time at North Head Lighthouse, a historic beacon perched on the edge of the Washington coast. This iconic lighthouse in Ilwaco is a testament to maritime history and offers a unique vista of the Pacific Ocean and the Columbia River.

Location: N Head Lighthouse Rd, Ilwaco, WA 98624

Closest City or Town: Ilwaco, Washington

How to Get There: From Ilwaco, head west on Elizabeth Ave toward 1st Ave S. Continue onto N Head Lighthouse Rd.

GPS Coordinates: 46.298456° N, 124.0655699° W

Best Time to Visit: Open all year round, but the best views are seen during the summer months.

Pass/Permit/Fees: There are fees for lighthouse tours.

Did You Know? The North Head Lighthouse has been guiding ships since 1898.

Website: http://northheadlighthouse.com/

LEAVENWORTH

Waterfront Park

Experience the beauty of the Bavarian Village of Leavenworth, Washington at Waterfront Park! Located at 500 9th St, this riverside park offers views of the Wenatchee River and a variety of recreational activities. Take a stroll down the riverside path, picnic under shady trees, or simply enjoy the fresh mountain air.

Location: 500 9th St, Leavenworth, WA 98826

Closest City or Town: Leavenworth, Washington

How to Get There: From downtown Leavenworth drive east on Highway 2 and turn left onto 9th Street. Park at the end of the road.

GPS Coordinates: 47.5944885° N, 120.659602° W

Best Time to Visit: Waterfront Park is open year-round and offers stunning views in all four seasons!

Pass/Permit/Fees: Entrance is free.

Did You Know? Waterfront Park is a popular spot for fishing, kayaking, and stand-up paddleboarding!

Website: http://cityofleavenworth.com/city-government/parks/waterfront-park

Leavenworth Reindeer Farm

Experience the magic of the Arctic right here in Washington State at the Leavenworth Reindeer Farm! Nestled in the stunning setting of Leavenworth, this farm offers you a singular opportunity to interact with real reindeer. Feed them, pet them, and learn about these exquisite creatures from the friendly and knowledgeable staff.

Location: 10395 Chumstick Hwy, Leavenworth, WA 98826-9285

Closest City or Town: Leavenworth, Washington

How to Get There: From Leavenworth, head north on Chumstick Hwy for about 4 miles. The farm will be on your right.

GPS Coordinates: 47.6066435° N, 120.6493273° W

Best Time to Visit: The farm is open year-round, but the experience is particularly magical during the winter months.

Pass/Permit/Fees: Entrance fees apply. Please visit their website for more details.

Did You Know? Leavenworth Reindeer Farm is one of the few places in the U.S. where you can have a hands-on experience with these incredible animals!

Website: http://www.experiencereindeer.com/

Front Street Park

Discover a slice of Bavaria in the heart of Washington at Front Street Park, located in the charming town of Leavenworth. The park serves as the town's focal point for community activities and events, offering breathtaking views of the surrounding mountains, an alpine garden, and a traditional Maibaum (maypole).

Location: 820 Front St, Leavenworth, WA 98826

Closest City or Town: Leavenworth, Washington

How to Get There: From US-2, turn onto Front Street and the park will be on your right.

GPS Coordinates: 47.5956179° N, 120.6618939° W

Best Time to Visit: Year-round, with activities changing with the seasons.

Pass/Permit/Fees: Free to visit

Did You Know? Leavenworth is a Bavarian-styled village in the Cascade Mountains, making Front Street Park a unique destination in the Pacific Northwest.

Website: http://www.leavenworth.org/experience/parks

Leavenworth Sleigh Rides

Step into a winter wonderland with Leavenworth Sleigh Rides, located on Chiwawa Loop Road in Leavenworth. Here, you can experience the magic of a traditional horse-drawn sleigh ride through the snow-covered forest. Remember to snuggle up under the provided blankets and enjoy the enchanting jingle of the sleigh bells!

Location: 19115 Chiwawa Loop Rd, Leavenworth, WA 98826-9550

Closest City or Town: Leavenworth, Washington

How to Get There: From Leavenworth, take US-2 E and turn right onto Chiwawa Loop Road. Follow the signs to reach the destination.

GPS Coordinates: 47.767185° N, 120.651658° W

Best Time to Visit: During the winter months when snow is abundant.

Pass/Permit/Fees: Rates vary depending on group size and day of the week, please visit the website for more details.

Did You Know? Leavenworth Sleigh Rides offers a unique and romantic way to experience the winter landscape of Leavenworth.

Website: https://www.leavenworthsleighrides.com/

Icicle Gorge

Immerse yourself in the scenic beauty of Icicle Gorge, nestled in the serene landscapes of Leavenworth, Washington. This natural oasis offers you the opportunity to hike along meandering trails, offering panoramic views of the stunning gorge. The area's unique feature is its breathtaking Icicle Creek, a perfect spot for fishing and wildlife viewing.

Location: J454+C5 Leavenworth, Washington

Closest City or Town: Leavenworth, Washington

How to Get There: From Leavenworth, follow US-2 W and WA-207 N to Icicle Rd. Follow Icicle Rd to the destination.

GPS Coordinates: 47.6085625° N, 120.8945625° W

Best Time to Visit: Spring to Fall, when the weather is pleasant for outdoor activities.

Pass/Permit/Fees: The destination is Free to visit.

Did You Know? Icicle Gorge derives its name from the Icicle Creek flowing through it, which offers abundant trout fishing opportunities.

Website: http://www.leavenworth.org/trail/icicle-gorge

LONG BEACH

Long Beach Boardwalk

Experience the unspoiled beauty of the Pacific Northwest at the Long Beach Boardwalk, nestled in the heart of Washington State. This long stretch of pristine beach is a haven for outdoor enthusiasts, with the Discovery Trail providing a scenic route for hiking and cycling. Enjoy stunning panoramic views of the ocean, and don't miss the chance to witness a breathtaking sunset. Unique to Long Beach, the Boardwalk offers an ideal spot for bird watching with the opportunity to spot numerous local and migratory species.

Location: Sands, Discovery Trail, Long Beach, WA 98631, United States

Closest City or Town: Long Beach, Washington (located within the city)

How to Get There: From the city center of Long Beach, head west onto Ocean Beach Blvd S. Continue on the boulevard until you reach the intersection with Discovery Trail, where you will find the entrance to the boardwalk.

GPS Coordinates: 46.3518149° N, 124.0656799° W

Best Time to Visit: Long Beach Boardwalk is open year-round, but the best time to visit is from late spring through early fall when the weather is most pleasant.

Pass/Permit/Fees: Free to enter

Did You Know? The Discovery Trail is a tribute to the Lewis and Clark expedition and features interpretative displays throughout the route, making history come alive for visitors.

Website: http://www.visitlongbeachpeninsula.com/things-to-do/beach/

LONGVIEW

Ape Cave Lava Tubes

Dive into an underground adventure at the Ape Cave Lava Tubes, a fascinating geological formation in Cougar, Washington. This subterranean marvel, nestled amidst the verdant landscapes, presents an opportunity to explore one of the longest lava tubes in North America. Don your headlamps and venture into the cool, dark depths for a one-of-a-kind caving experience.

Location: 24000 Spirit Lake Hwy, Cougar, WA 98616

Closest City or Town: Cougar, Washington

How to Get There: From Cougar, take the Lewis River Road east. Turn left onto NF-83 and continue until you reach the Ape Cave parking area.

GPS Coordinates: 46.2752681° N, 122.2172109° W

Best Time to Visit: Spring through fall.

Pass/Permit/Fees: Northwest Forest Pass required ($5/day or $30/year).

Did You Know? The caves were named after the amateur explorers who first discovered them, members of the St. Helens Apes.

Website: http://mountsthelens.com/ape-caves.html

MARYSVILLE

Seattle Premium Outlets

Experience shopping at its finest at Seattle Premium Outlets. Located in Marysville, this outlet mall offers an array of high-end retail stores, where you can snag some great deals. Whether you're looking for designer fashion or homewares, or just want to indulge in a bit of retail therapy, this is the place to be.

Location: 10600 Quil Ceda Blvd, Marysville, WA 98271

Closest City or Town: Marysville, Washington

How to Get There: From I-5 take exit 202 for 116th St NE, then turn west onto 116th St NE, and finally turn right onto Quil Ceda Blvd.

GPS Coordinates: 48.0927799° N, 122.1890947° W

Best Time to Visit: Open year-round, but the holiday season is particularly lively with special events and sales.

Pass/Permit/Fees: Free admission, but individual stores may have their own pricing.

Did You Know? The outlet is partly owned by the Tulalip Tribes of Washington and features native art throughout its premises.

Website: http://www.premiumoutlets.com/outlet/seattle

MOUNT RAINIER NATIONAL PARK

Grove of the Patriarchs

Step back in time at the Grove of the Patriarchs. This ancient grove located in Mount Rainier National Park, Washington, boasts centuries-old trees that have stood the test of time, offering a spellbinding journey through the history and grandeur of nature.

Location: QC5V+73 Packwood, Washington

Closest City or Town: Packwood, Washington

How to Get There: From Packwood, head northeast towards the Mount Rainier National Park entrance. Follow the signs to the Grove of the Patriarchs.

GPS Coordinates: 46.7581875° N, 121.5573125° W

Best Time to Visit: Year-round, but the grove is especially beautiful in summer.

Pass/Permit/Fees: $30 per vehicle for a day pass.

Did You Know? The Grove is home to gigantic trees that are over 1,000 years old.

Website: http://www.wta.org/go-hiking/hikes/grove-of-the-patriarchs

Skyline Trail

Prepare for a captivating journey on the Skyline Trail, a popular hiking route in the stunning Mount Rainier National Park. The trail offers an unforgettable adventure through alpine meadows, past cascading waterfalls, and around glacier-fed lakes. At an elevation of over 6,000 feet, the trail provides breathtaking panoramic views of Mount Rainier and the surrounding landscape. Don't forget to look for the abundant wildflowers that bloom along the trail in the summer!

Location: Paradise Rd E, Ashford, WA 98304 (Visitor Center)

Closest City or Town: Ashford, Washington

How to Get There: From Ashford, head northwest on WA-7 towards Mount Rainier National Park. Take a right onto Paradise Rd E, and the visitor center will be on your left.

GPS Coordinates: 46.7538884° N, 121.8129819° W

Best Time to Visit: The trail is best enjoyed in the summer or fall months when temperatures are warmer and the wildflowers are in full bloom.**Pass/Permit/Fees:** No fees or passes are required for entry to the park, but a national parks pass may be necessary for certain attractions.

Did You Know? The Skyline Trail is named after its spectacular views of Mount Rainier, which can be seen from many points along the way.

Website: http://www.nps.gov/mora/planyourvisit/skyline-trail.htm

Sunrise Visitor Center

Sunrise Visitor Center is your gateway to majestic views and unforgettable experiences in Mount Rainier National Park. Located at Sunrise, the highest point in the park accessible by vehicle, it offers unparalleled vistas of Mount Rainier and Emmons Glacier. Explore the day-use area with hiking trails, a visitor center, and a picnic area. Don't miss the stunning sunrise that bathes the landscape in breathtaking hues!

Location: Sunrise Park Rd, Ashford, WA 98304

Closest City or Town: Ashford, Washington (approximately 60 miles to the southwest)

How to Get There: From Ashford, follow SR 706 E (which becomes Paradise Rd E), make a right onto Sunrise Rd, and follow it to the end.

GPS Coordinates: 46.90208° N, 121.598661° W

Best Time to Visit: Open daily from July through September (weather permitting).

Pass/Permit/Fees: A standard amenity fee applies for the use of the day-use recreation sites. Visit the website for specific rates.

Did You Know? Sunrise Visitor Center is named for the breathtaking sunrises that can be witnessed here - truly a sight to behold!

Website: http://www.nps.gov/mora/planyourvisit/sunrise.htm

MOUNT VERNON

Roozengaarde Display Garden

Immerse yourself in a riot of color at the Roozengaarde Display Garden, located in the scenic Skagit Valley of Mount Vernon, Washington. Home to lush tulip fields, the garden is a floral wonderland that will leave you spellbound. From the picturesque bulb fields to the Dutch windmill, there's something for everyone here!

Location: 15867 Beaver Marsh Rd, Mount Vernon, WA 98273-8802

Closest City or Town: Mount Vernon, Washington

How to Get There: From I-5 N, take exit 230 for WA-20 toward Burlington/Anacortes. Turn left onto WA-20 W, then turn right onto Beaver Marsh Rd.

GPS Coordinates: 48.4156586° N, 122.4000531° W

Best Time to Visit: The tulip bloom in the spring (April) is a sight to behold.

Pass/Permit/Fees: Admission fees apply, please visit their website for more details.

Did You Know? The Roozengaarde Display Garden houses more than 1,000,000 bulbs and is the only tulip garden in Washington.

Website: http://www.tulips.com/

MUKILTEO

Mukilteo Lighthouse Park

Bask in the tranquility of Mukilteo Lighthouse Park, a quiet escape nestled on the coast of Washington. This beautiful park, located in Mukilteo, offers a serene environment where you can enjoy a picnic or take a peaceful stroll by the waterfront. Don't forget to visit the iconic Mukilteo Lighthouse for a glimpse into history!

Location: 609 Front St, Mukilteo, WA 98275-1557

Closest City or Town: Mukilteo, Washington

How to Get There: From I-5, take exit 182 and follow signs for Mukilteo. Once in town, follow signs to the waterfront.

GPS Coordinates: 47.9487555° N, 122.3062009° W

Best Time to Visit: Spring through fall for the best weather.

Pass/Permit/Fees: Free entry to the park and lighthouse

Did You Know? The lighthouse is still operational and guided tours are available on weekends during the summer.

Website: http://mukilteowa.gov/departments/recreation/parks-open-spaces-trails/lighthouse-park/

NEAH BAY

Cape Flattery Trail

Welcome to the Cape Flattery Trail, where the magic of nature unfolds at every step. Located at the most northwestern point of the contiguous United States, this trail offers a tranquil retreat into the lush landscape of the Olympic Peninsula. Experience the thrill of the hiking trail that winds through forests and leads to a dramatic vista overlooking the Pacific Ocean. An observation deck offers stunning views of the sea and the distant Tatoosh Island, a unique feature of this location.

Location: Cape Loop Rd, Neah Bay, WA 98357

Closest City or Town: Neah Bay, Washington (located within the city)

How to Get There: From Neah Bay, take Cape Loop Rd westward out of town. Follow the road for about 8 miles, and the trailhead will be on the left.

GPS Coordinates: 48.3744764° N, 124.6329629° W

Best Time to Visit: Open year-round, but the best time to visit is from May to September when the weather is most enjoyable for hiking.

Pass/Permit/Fees: Free to enter

Did You Know? The trail is located on the Makah Reservation, and the Makah Tribe has called this area home for over 3,500 years.

Website: http://northolympic.com/files/capeflatterytrail/index.htm

Makah Cultural and Research Center

Journey through time at the Makah Cultural and Research Center in Neah Bay, Washington. The center showcases the rich history and culture of the Makah Indian Tribe through a variety of exhibits, artifacts, and educational programs. A unique feature is a replica of a Makah longhouse, which provides a glimpse into the tribe's traditional way of life.

Location: 1880 Bayview Ave, Neah Bay, WA 98357

WASHINGTON BUCKET LIST

Closest City or Town: Neah Bay, Washington

How to Get There: From downtown Neah Bay, head east on Bayview Ave. The destination will be on the right.

GPS Coordinates: 48.3682702° N, 124.598673° W

Best Time to Visit: The center is open year-round, but spring to fall are the busiest seasons.

Pass/Permit/Fees: General admission is $6 for adults, $5 for seniors, $4 for students, and free for children 5 and under.

Did You Know? The center houses over 300,000 artifacts and samples dating back to 500 BC!

Website: http://www.makahmuseum.com/

NORTH CASCADES NATIONAL PARK

North Cascades Highway

Set off for an unforgettable adventure along the North Cascades Highway. This scenic byway, part of the Washington State Route 20, offers travelers a breathtaking journey through the heart of the North Cascades National Park. The highway winds through rugged mountain landscapes, lush forest valleys, and past crystal-clear alpine lakes, offering countless opportunities for hiking, photography, and wildlife viewing. One ride on this highway and you will understand why it is considered one of the most beautiful roads in America!

Location: 810 State Route 20, Sedro-Woolley, WA 98284 (Visitor Center)

Closest City or Town: Sedro-Woolley, Washington

How to Get There: From Interstate 5, take the exit for WA-20 east (exit 230). Follow WA-20 east towards Sedro-Woolley, and the visitor center will be on your right.

GPS Coordinates: 48.5109572° N, 122.2276015° W

Best Time to Visit: Late spring to early fall, when the road is free of snow and the weather is pleasant.

Pass/Permit/Fees: No fees or passes are required to drive the highway, but individual attractions along the route may charge fees.

Did You Know? North Cascades Highway is the northernmost route across the Cascades in Washington and offers stunning views of the range.

Website: http://www.seattle.gov/light/tours/skagit

Diablo Lake Overlook

Prepare to be amazed at Diablo Lake Overlook, nestled in the stunning Pacific Northwest region of Washington State. This iconic viewing point, located along the North Cascades Highway, offers unparalleled views of the turquoise Diablo Lake against the backdrop of the majestic North Cascade mountains. Adventure enthusiasts can indulge in a multitude of recreational activities, including hiking, paddling, and wildlife viewing. The Overlook's standout feature is undoubtedly its awe-inspiring vista, which appears more like a captivating painting than a real-life landscape.

Location: PW53+X2 Diablo, Washington, United States

Closest City or Town: Newhalem, Washington (a short drive away)

How to Get There: From Newhalem, take WA-20 E/N Cascades Hwy for about 10 miles. The Diablo Lake Overlook will be on your right.

GPS Coordinates: 48.7101983° N, 121.0974069° W

Best Time to Visit: Summer months, between June and September, are the optimal time for viewing the vibrant lake colors and engaging in recreational activities.

Pass/Permit/Fees: The overlook is free to visit, but certain activities may require fees.

Did You Know? Diablo Lake's distinctive turquoise color is due to glacial silt from the surrounding mountains reflecting sunlight, creating a mesmerizing effect.

Website: https://www.nps.gov/noca/planyourvisit/accessibility-at-diablo-lake-overlook.htm

OAK HARBOR

Deception Pass State Park

Take in the breathtaking scenery of Deception Pass State Park, a stunning marine and camping park located on Whidbey Island, Washington. The park's unique features include the Deception Pass Bridge, rugged cliffs, and spectacular views of the turbulent waters of Deception Pass.

Location: 5175 N State Hwy 20, Oak Harbor, Whidbey Island, WA 98277

Closest City or Town: Oak Harbor, Whidbey Island, Washington

How to Get There: From Oak Harbor, head south on Hwy 20, follow signs to the park.

GPS Coordinates: 48.4181986° N, 122.6328894° W

Best Time to Visit: The park is open year-round but the summer months (June - August) are ideal for all activities.

Pass/Permit/Fees: The park charges a daily vehicle entrance fee, but no other pass or permit is required.

Did You Know? Deception Pass State Park is Washington's most visited state park, with over 2 million people each year!

Website: http://parksguidance.com/deception-pass-state-park/

OCEAN SHORES

North Jetty

Witness the power of nature at the North Jetty. Located in Ocean Shores, Washington, the Jetty offers the thrilling spectacle of crashing waves and the opportunity to explore marine life in tide pools. This rugged stretch of coastline is a haven for bird watchers, photographers, and those seeking a tranquil retreat.

Location: WRHG+MQ Ocean Shores, Washington

Closest City or Town: Ocean Shores, Washington

How to Get There: From Ocean Shores, head west on Chance a La Mer NW. Turn right onto Ocean Shores Blvd NW, then a left onto Marine View Dr. SW. Follow signs to the Jetty.

GPS Coordinates: 46.9291875° N, 124.1730625° W

Best Time to Visit: Open year-round, but the summer months offer the best weather for exploring.

Pass/Permit/Fees: Free.

Did You Know? The North Jetty is the perfect spot to watch winter storms roll in off the Pacific.

Website: http://cityofoceanshores.com/the-north-jetty

Coastal Interpretive Center

Discover the natural and cultural history of Ocean Shores at the Coastal Interpretive Center. From Native American artifacts to local wildlife exhibits, the center offers an educational and interactive experience for all ages. Don't miss the earthquake simulator for an exciting hands-on experience!

Location: 1033 Catala Ave SE Corner of Catala Ave and Discovery Ave., Ocean Shores, WA 98569-9761

Closest City or Town: Ocean Shores, Washington

How to Get There: From Aberdeen, take WA-109 N for about 20 miles. Turn right onto Discovery Ave and then left onto Catala Ave.

GPS Coordinates: 46.9521047° N, 124.1319559° W

Best Time to Visit: Open year-round but summer is the best time to combine with a beach trip.

Pass/Permit/Fees: Free entrance, donations are appreciated.

Did You Know? The Coastal Interpretive Center is the only interpretive facility on North Beach.

Website: http://interpretivecenter.org/

OLGA

Moran State Park

Immerse yourself in Mother Nature's lap at Moran State Park, located on the tranquil Orcas Island. The park is home to over 5,000 acres of wilderness, 38 miles of hiking trails, and the captivating Cascade Falls. Whether you're camping under the stars or climbing to the top of Mount Constitution, the highest point in the San Juan Islands, the beauty of the park is sure to leave you spellbound.

Location: 3572 Olga Rd, Olga, Orcas Island, WA 98279-8556

Closest City or Town: Eastsound, Washington

How to Get There: The park is accessible via the Washington State Ferries from Anacortes to Orcas Island. After arriving on the island, follow Orcas Road and turn right onto Olga Road.

GPS Coordinates: 48.6572404° N, 122.8587941° W

Best Time to Visit: The park is open year-round, but the best time to visit is from April to October.

Pass/Permit/Fees: A Discover Pass is required for vehicle access to the park ($30 annual or $10 one-day).

Did You Know? The park was named after Robert Moran, a shipbuilder and former mayor of Seattle, who donated the land for the park.

Website: https://www.parks.wa.gov/547/Moran

OLYMPIA

Nisqually National Wildlife Refuge

Immerse yourself in the tranquil beauty of the Nisqually National Wildlife Refuge, a sanctuary teeming with diverse wildlife and unique ecosystems. Situated near Olympia, Washington, this haven offers breathtaking views and a range of recreational activities for all nature lovers.

Location: 100 Brown Farm Rd NE, Olympia, WA 98516-2302

Closest City or Town: Olympia, Washington

How to Get There: From downtown Olympia take US-101 N until you reach the Brown Farm Rd exit. Turn left onto Brown Farm Rd and follow it until you reach the entrance of the refuge.

GPS Coordinates: 47.0727679° N, 122.7127309° W

Best Time to Visit: Spring and Fall months are the best time for visiting as temperatures tend to be milder during that season.

Pass/Permit/Fees: Entrance is free but you must purchase a permit if you wish to hunt or fish in the refuge.

Did You Know? The Nisqually National Wildlife Refuge is a popular spot for bird-watchers, especially during the spring and fall migrations.

Website:
http://www.fws.gov/refuge/Billy_Frank_Jr_Nisqually/visit/plan_your_visit.html

Washington State Capitol

Experience a blend of history and architecture at the Washington State Capitol. Located in Olympia, the building is notable for its distinctive dome, one of the largest free-standing masonry domes in the world. From guided tours to picturesque gardens, there's something for everyone.

Location: 416 Sid Snyder Ave SW, Olympia, WA 98501-1347

Closest City or Town: Olympia, Washington

How to Get There: From Olympia, head south on Capitol Way S, then turn right onto 14th Ave SW. Turn left onto Sid Snyder Ave SW to reach the Capitol.

GPS Coordinates: 47.0359422° N, 122.9044453° W

Best Time to Visit: Year-round, but spring offers the added allure of cherry blossoms.

Pass/Permit/Fees: Free, but guided tours may have a nominal fee.

Did You Know? The building's chandelier, weighing 10,000 pounds, is the largest to be found in any public building in the US.

Website: http://olympiawa.gov/community/visiting-the-capitol.aspx

Hands-On Children's Museum

Spark your child's imagination at the Hands On Children's Museum in Olympia, Washington. This state-of-the-art facility is designed to stimulate creativity, curiosity, and a love of learning through playful explorations in interactive exhibit galleries. From art to science, your little ones will have a blast while learning.

Location: 414 Jefferson St NE, Olympia, WA 98501-1124

Closest City or Town: Olympia, Washington

How to Get There: From downtown Olympia, head east on 4th Ave E. Turn left onto Jefferson St NE. The museum will be on your right.

GPS Coordinates: 47.0480478° N, 122.8965656° W

Best Time to Visit: Open year-round, check the website for special events and exhibits.

Pass/Permit/Fees: Fees apply, with discounts for members and children under age 2.

Did You Know? The museum offers free admission every first Friday of the month from 5pm - 9pm.

Website: http://www.hocm.org/

Olympia Farmers Market

Experience the buzz of a bustling market at the Olympia Farmers Market. This vibrant marketplace located in Olympia, Washington, offers a plethora of fresh local produce, handmade crafts, and food stalls. It's a perfect place to pick up unique souvenirs and taste authentic local flavors.

Location: 700 Capitol Way S, Olympia, WA 98501-1208

Closest City or Town: Olympia, Washington

How to Get There: From I-5 S, take exit 105 for Port of Olympia. Keep right at the fork, follow the signs for City Center.

GPS Coordinates: 47.04217° N, 122.901252° W

Best Time to Visit: Open year-round, but the summer months bring a wider variety of products.

Pass/Permit/Fees: Free to visit, but bring some cash for shopping!

Did You Know? The Olympia Farmers Market is one of the largest markets in Washington State with over 100 vendors.

Website: http://www.olympiafarmersmarket.com/

Percival Landing

Experience the vibrant waterfront life at Percival Landing, located in Olympia, Washington. This public park is the perfect destination to enjoy a leisurely stroll along the boardwalk, take in spectacular views of the marina, and explore the local shops and restaurants. Its unique feature is the collection of public art installations scattered throughout the park.

Location: 217 Thurston Ave NE, Olympia, WA 98501-1171

Closest City or Town: Olympia, Washington

How to Get There: From downtown Olympia, head east on 4th ave towards Cherry St SE. Continue onto Thurston Ave NE and the destination will be on the right.

GPS Coordinates: 47.0475624° N, 122.9001859° W

Best Time to Visit: The park is open year-round, but summer is the most popular time to visit.

Pass/Permit/Fees: Free entry.

Did You Know? Percival Landing hosts the annual Olympia Harbor Days, an arts and crafts festival that celebrates the maritime heritage of South Puget Sound.

Website: http://olympiawa.gov/community/parks/percival-landing.aspx

OLYMPIC NATIONAL PARK

Hoh Rain Forest

Embark on the journey of a lifetime in the verdant Hoh Rainforest. Nestled within the sprawling Olympic National Park in Washington State, this evergreen sanctuary offers a unique and immersive nature experience. Discover the enchanting Hall of Mosses, explore the winding trails under the towering trees, and enjoy in the sights and sounds of the diverse wildlife. The forest's lush, green beauty and tranquil silence are truly mesmerizing.

Location: 18113 Upper Hoh Rd, Forks, WA 98331 (Visitor Center)

Closest City or Town: Forks, Washington

How to Get There: From US-101 in Forks, turn onto Upper Hoh Rd. Follow this road for about an hour, and you will reach the visitor center.

GPS Coordinates: 47.8608809° N, 123.9348334° W

Best Time to Visit: Spring and summer are ideal for taking advantage of the milder weather and vibrant greenery.

Pass/Permit/Fees: The entrance fee for Olympic National Park is $30 per vehicle, with various passes available.

Did You Know? The Hoh Rain Forest is one of the largest temperate rainforests in the U.S., allowing a vast array of flora and fauna to flourish.

Website: http://www.nps.gov/olym/planyourvisit/visiting-the-hoh.htm

Ruby Beach

Experience the mesmerizing allure of Ruby Beach, one of the crown jewels of Washington's Pacific coastline. This unspoiled paradise offers awe-inspiring sunsets, dramatic seascapes, and the chance to encounter diverse wildlife.

Location: Ruby Beach, Forks, WA 98331

Closest City or Town: Forks, Washington

How to Get There: From US-101, turn onto Ruby Beach Road, and follow it to the end for the parking area.

GPS Coordinates: 47.7108733° N, 124.4154024° W

Best Time to Visit: Summer months provide the best weather and viewing conditions for wildlife.

Pass/Permit/Fees: No entrance fee is required.

Did You Know? The beach got its name from the ruby-like crystals found in the beach sand.

Website: http://www.nps.gov/olym/planyourvisit/visiting-kalaloch-and-ruby-beach.htm

Lake Crescent

Let the enchanting beauty of Lake Crescent captivate you. Cradled in the Olympic National Park in Washington, this deepwater lake offers breathtaking vistas and myriad recreational activities. From hiking, swimming to fishing – Lake Crescent offers an idyllic retreat into nature.

Location: Lake Crescent Rd, Olympic National Park, WA 98363

Closest City or Town: Port Angeles, Washington

How to Get There: From Port Angeles, head west on US-101. Turn right onto E Beach Rd, then left onto Lake Crescent Rd.

GPS Coordinates: 48.0576567° N, 123.7932216° W

Best Time to Visit: Spring to fall

Pass/Permit/Fees: Free, but a National Park pass is required

Did You Know? Lake Crescent is recognized for its bright blue waters and excellent clarity due to a nitrogen deficiency that prevents algae growth!

Website: https://www.nps.gov/olym/planyourvisit/visiting-lake-crescent.htm

Rialto Beach

Rialto Beach, situated on the Pacific Coast of Washington, offers a serene escape into nature's grandeur. This beach is renowned for its captivating rock formations and driftwood-strewn shorelines. Visitors can enjoy the rhythmic crashing of waves, go tide pooling, or simply wander along the beach, observing the marine life and birds. Don't miss the opportunity to witness a magical sunset here!

Location: Mora Rd, Forks, WA 98350

Closest City or Town: Forks, Washington

How to Get There: From Forks, take US-101 S and State Route 110 to Mora Rd. Follow Mora Rd directly to Rialto Beach.

GPS Coordinates: 47.9176347° N, 124.5862987° W

Best Time to Visit: Year-round, but summer and fall offer the best weather conditions.

Pass/Permit/Fees: Free. No passes or fees are required.

Did You Know? Rialto Beach is one of the few places in the world where you can witness "marine stacks" - a unique geological formation of isolated rock pillars.

Website: http://www.nps.gov/olym/planyourvisit/rialto-beach.htm

Olympic National Forest

Experience the majestic beauty of the Olympic National Forest. Located on Washington's Olympic Peninsula, this expansive forest is a haven for outdoor enthusiasts. Indulge in an array of activities like hiking, fishing, camping, or wildlife watching, and experience the forest's unique ecosystem. The panoramic views of mountains, rivers, and forests are awe-inspiring!

Location: 3002 Mount Angeles Rd, Port Angeles, WA 98362-6775 (Visitor Center)

Closest City or Town: Port Angeles, Washington

How to Get There: From Port Angeles, head south on S Lincoln St toward E Lauridsen Blvd. Turn right at the 1st cross street onto E Front

St, and then turn left onto Mount Angeles Rd. The visitor center will be on your right.

GPS Coordinates: 48.0993011° N, 123.4256899° W

Best Time to Visit: Late spring to early fall when the weather is most suitable for outdoor activities.

Pass/Permit/Fees: Forest entry is free, but recreational passes may be required for certain activities like camping and hiking.

Did You Know? The forest is home to five different vegetation zones, hosting an impressive biodiversity.

Website: http://www.fs.usda.gov/olympic/

Sol Duc Falls

Venture into the lush wilderness of Olympic National Park at Sol Duc Falls, a breathtakingly beautiful cascade tucked into a verdant old-growth forest. Located at 12076 Sol Duc-Hot Springs Rd, Port Angeles, this waterfall promises a refreshing escape into nature's tranquility.

Location: 12076 Sol Duc-Hot Springs Rd, Port Angeles, WA 98363

Closest City or Town: Port Angeles, Washington

How to Get There: Take US-101 N from Port Angeles and follow Sol Duc Hot Springs Rd to the parking lot.

GPS Coordinates: 47.9689738° N, 123.863° W

Best Time to Visit: Summer months are the best time for visiting, as the temperatures tend to be milder during that season.

Pass/Permit/Fees: Entrance is free.

Did You Know? Sol Duc Falls has been used in many films and TV shows due to its incredible beauty!

Website: http://www.nps.gov/olym/planyourvisit/visiting-the-sol-duc-valley.htm

Second Beach Trail

Discover the magic of Washington's rugged coastline on the Second Beach Trail. Starting from the town of La Push, this trail will take you through lush forests to a breathtaking coastline adorned with sea stacks. Experience the tranquil ambiance of the Pacific Northwest as you explore this scenic trail.

Location: Olympic Discovery Trail, La Push, WA 98350

Closest City or Town: La Push, Washington

How to Get There: From Forks, take US-101 N, then turn left onto La Push Rd. Follow La Push Rd to the trailhead.

GPS Coordinates: 47.8983053° N, 124.6213044° W

Best Time to Visit: Summer months, when the weather is dry and warm, are the best time to hit the trail.

Pass/Permit/Fees: No fees are required to hike the trail.

Did You Know? Second Beach is the most photographed beach in Olympic National Park!

Website: http://www.nps.gov/olym/planyourvisit/second-beach-trail.htm

Quinault Rain Forest

Step into a world of lush greenery and tranquility at the Quinault Rain Forest, located in the heart of the Olympic National Park. With its towering trees, cascading waterfalls, and diverse wildlife, this temperate rainforest offers an enchanting escape from the modern world. Experience the serenity and peace that only untouched natural beauty can provide.

Location: 4Q5Q+686 Cougar, Washington

Closest City or Town: Cougar, Washington

How to Get There: From U.S. Highway 101, turn onto South Shore Road near the town of Amanda Park.

GPS Coordinates: 46.1080374° N, 122.2117344° W

Best Time to Visit: Year-round, with each season offering a unique experience.

Pass/Permit/Fees: $30 vehicle fee for a 7-day Olympic National Park pass.

WASHINGTON BUCKET LIST

Did You Know? The forest is home to the world's largest Sitka Spruce tree, standing at 191 feet tall.

Website: http://www.quinaultrainforest.com/

PORT ANGELES

Black Ball Ferry Line

Discover the maritime beauty of Washington's scenic coastline aboard the Black Ball Ferry Line. This charming vessel departs from Port Angeles and cruises to Victoria, British Columbia, offering stunning views of the Olympic Mountains and the Strait of Juan de Fuca.

Location: 101 E Railroad Ave, Port Angeles, WA 98362-2912

Closest City or Town: Port Angeles, Washington

How to Get There: The ferry is located at The Landing Mall in downtown Port Angeles.

GPS Coordinates: 48.1209402° N, 123.4316587° W

Best Time to Visit: The ferry runs from March through October each year. **Pass/Permit/Fees:** One-way fares range from $18 to $35 depending on the destination.

Did You Know? The ferry is a continuation of a steamer service that dates back to the 1850s!

Website: http://www.blackballferryline.com/

Marymere Falls

Find tranquility in nature at Marymere Falls, nestled in the heart of Olympic National Park. Here, you can marvel at the waterfall cascading from a height of 90 feet into a small, serene pool. The hike to the waterfall threads its way through a beautiful forest, a journey just as breathtaking as the destination itself.

Location: Lake Crescent Rd, Port Angeles, WA 98363, United States

Closest City or Town: Port Angeles, Washington

How to Get There: From Port Angeles, take US-101 W to Lake Crescent Rd, then a short hike leads to the falls.

GPS Coordinates: 48.0576567° N, 123.7932216° W

Best Time to Visit: Spring and early summer when the waterfall is at its most voluminous.

Pass/Permit/Fees: National Park pass required.

Did You Know? The trail to Marymere Falls passes through one of the last remaining old-growth forests in the United States.

Website: http://www.wta.org/go-hiking/hikes/marymere-falls

Salt Creek Recreation Area

Reconnect with nature at the Salt Creek Recreation Area, an expansive wildlife sanctuary located in Port Angeles, Washington. With a diverse landscape of forests, tidal pools, and sandy beaches, it's a haven for outdoor enthusiasts. Don't miss the stunning views of the Strait of Juan de Fuca and Victoria, British Columbia from the top of the bluffs!

Location: 3506 Camp Hayden Rd, Port Angeles, WA 98363-8702

Closest City or Town: Port Angeles, Washington

How to Get There: From Port Angeles, head west on US-101 until you turn left onto Camp Hayden Rd. Continue until you reach the park entrance.

GPS Coordinates: 48.1658354° N, 123.704217° W

Best Time to Visit: Year-round, with peak season during the summer months.

Pass/Permit/Fees: A Discover Pass is required for vehicle access.

Did You Know? The Salt Creek Recreation Area was once Camp Hayden, a World War II military camp.

Website: http://www.clallam.net/Parks/SaltCreek.html

PORT TOWNSEND

Fort Worden State Park

Immerse yourself in the natural beauty and rich history of Fort Worden State Park, located in Port Townsend, Washington. Here, history buffs can explore military installations and bunkers, while nature lovers can enjoy scenic hiking trails and breathtaking waterfront views. The park is unique in its combination of natural beauty and historical significance, promising a diverse and enriching experience for all visitors.

Location: 200 Battery Way, Port Townsend, WA 98368-3621

Closest City or Town: Port Townsend, Washington

How to Get There: Head northwest on WA-20 from downtown Port Townsend. Make a slight left onto Cherry St and then turn right onto Eisenhower Ave. Continue onto Battery Way and you will reach the park.

GPS Coordinates: 48.1345059° N, 122.7650915° W

Best Time to Visit: Open year-round, but the summer months are particularly enjoyable for outdoor activities.

Pass/Permit/Fees: A Discover Pass is required for vehicle access to state parks for day use. For more details on fees, check the park's website.

Did You Know? Fort Worden was originally designed as a military base to protect Puget Sound from potential invasions.

Website: http://www.parks.wa.gov/511/Fort-Worden

Chetzemoka Park

Experience the charm of Port Townsend at Chetzemoka Park. Named after a respected Native American chief, this nine-acre park is a perfect spot for a family outing. Enjoy the beautiful gardens, playgrounds, picnic areas, and views of Admiralty Inlet and the Cascade and Olympic Mountains. Don't forget to visit the historic Jackson House, located within the park.

Location: 1000 Jackson St, Port Townsend, WA 98368

Closest City or Town: Port Townsend, Washington

How to Get There: From Port Townsend center, drive south on WA-20, turn left onto Kearney St, and then right onto Blaine St. Turn left onto Jackson St and continue till you reach the park.

GPS Coordinates: 48.1215939° N, 122.7557314° W

Best Time to Visit: The park is beautiful year-round, but spring and summer bring blooming flowers.

Pass/Permit/Fees: Free entrance.

Did You Know? Chetzemoka Park was the first public park to be established in Port Townsend in 1904.

Website: http://www.city-data.com/articles/Chetzemoka-Park-Port-Townsend-Washington.html

QUINAULT

Rain Forest Nature Trail

Embark on a serene journey through the lush landscapes of the Rain Forest Nature Trail. This trail in Quinault, Washington, is nestled within the verdant wilderness of the Olympic National Forest, offering a tranquil escape replete with towering trees, moss carpets, and melodious bird song.

Location: F45Q+W3 Quinault, Washington

Closest City or Town: Quinault, Washington

How to Get There: From Quinault, follow the signs to the Olympic National Forest and the Rain Forest Nature Trail.

GPS Coordinates: 47.4598125° N, 123.8623125° W

Best Time to Visit: Year-round, but spring and summer offer the most vibrant plant life.

Pass/Permit/Fees: Free entrance.

Did You Know? The Olympic National Forest is home to some of the largest trees in the world.

Website: http://www.fs.usda.gov/recarea/olympic/recarea/

REDMOND

Marymoor Park

Nestled on the north end of Lake Sammamish in Redmond, Washington, Marymoor Park offers 640 acres of picturesque scenery and outdoor fun. This park is the perfect playground for all ages, with features like climbing rocks, a dog park, a community garden, and even a velodrome for track cycling. Don't miss the summer concerts; they're a unique feature of this vibrant park.

Location: 6046 W Lake Sammamish Pkwy NE, Redmond, WA 98052-4801

Closest City or Town: Redmond, Washington

How to Get There: From Redmond, take SR-520 E and exit onto W Lake Sammamish Pkwy NE. Follow the signs to the park.

GPS Coordinates: 47.6594346° N, 122.1087919° W

Best Time to Visit: Open year-round, but spring and summer are the best times to enjoy outdoor activities.

Pass/Permit/Fees: Parking fees apply; check their website for details.

Did You Know? Marymoor Park is King County's largest and most popular park, attracting more than 3 million visitors per year!

Website: http://www.marymooramphitheatre.com/

RENTON

Jimi Hendrix Grave Site

Pay your respects at the Jimi Hendrix Grave Site, located in Renton, Washington. The rock legend's final resting place features a beautiful granite dome memorial, a fitting tribute to one of the most influential guitarists and musicians of the 20th century.

Location: 350 Monroe Ave NE Greenwood Memorial Park, Renton, WA 98056-4151

Closest City or Town: Renton, Washington

How to Get There: From downtown Renton, take Logan Ave N to N 6th St. Turn right onto Monroe Ave NE to reach Greenwood Memorial Park.

GPS Coordinates: 47.4881096° N, 122.174325° W

Best Time to Visit: Open year-round

Pass/Permit/Fees: Admission is free

Did You Know? The Jimi Hendrix Memorial is visited by fans from all around the world, making it a must-visit for music lovers.

Website: http://www.jimihendrixmemorial.com/

SEATTLE

Chihuly Garden and Glass

Immerse yourself in the vibrant world of glass art at the Chihuly Garden and Glass exhibition. Located in the heart of Seattle, this museum showcases the ingenious creations of Dale Chihuly, a world-renowned glass artist. Wander through the mesmerizing Glasshouse, the garden filled with intricate glass sculptures, and the eight galleries featuring Chihuly's significant series of works. The unique feature here is the 100-foot-long sculpture housed in the Glasshouse, one of Chihuly's largest suspended sculptures.

Location: 305 Harrison Street, Seattle, WA 98109-4623

Closest City or Town: Seattle, Washington (Located within the city)

How to Get There: From downtown Seattle, head north on 2nd Avenue. Turn left onto Denny Way and continue until you reach the Seattle Center. Chihuly Garden and Glass is right next to the iconic Space Needle.

GPS Coordinates 47.6228059° N, 122.353007° W

Best Time to Visit: Open year-round, but the spring and summer seasons when the garden is in full bloom offers the most magnificent views.

Pass/Permit/Fees: Tickets range from $19-$23.

Did You Know? Dale Chihuly, the artist behind the exhibits, is actually from Tacoma, Washington, just south of Seattle.

Website: http://www.chihulygardenandglass.com/

Pike Place Market

Discover the vibrant and bustling atmosphere of Seattle's oldest public market at Pike Place. Located in downtown Seattle, this historic marketplace is a celebration of local farmers, craftsmen, businesses, and artisans from around the region. Wander through stalls overflowing with fresh produce, gourmet cheeses, artisanal baked goods, and handcrafted souvenirs. The unique feature here is the iconic fish markets, which attract visitors from around the world with their lively and entertaining fish-tossing shows.

Location: 85 Pike St, Seattle, WA 98101

Closest City or Town: Seattle, Washington (Located within the city)

How to Get There: From downtown Seattle, head west on Pike Street. The market is located on the left, right before you reach the waterfront...

GPS Coordinates 47.6095222° N, 122.3421893° W

Best Time to Visit: The best time to visit is in the summer months when the market is at its most vibrant and lively with an abundance of fresh produce on display.

Pass/Permit/Fees: Admission is free, however, some stalls may charge for certain items.

Did You Know? Pike Place Market was established in 1907 and today continues to be one of the oldest continuously operating public markets in the US!

Website: http://pikeplacemarket.org/

Space Needle

Experience the city from a unique perspective at Seattle's iconic Space Needle. Located at the heart of the Seattle Center, this observation tower offers breathtaking panoramic views of downtown and the surrounding mountains. Ascend to the top via the elevators and take in views of Mt Rainier and other local landmarks. A unique feature here is the rotating SkyCity restaurant located at the top that makes a full rotation every 47 minutes.

Location: 400 Broad Street, Seattle, WA 98109-4607

Closest City or Town: Seattle, Washington (Located within the city)

How to Get There: The Space Needle is located in downtown Seattle and easily accessible via public transportation or driving.

GPS Coordinates 47.6203953° N, 122.3493709° W

Best Time to Visit: Head north on 2nd Avenue from downtown Seattle. Turn left on Broad Street. The Space Needle will be on your right.

Pass/Permit/Fees: Admission prices range from $19-$34.

Did You Know? The Space Needle was built for the 1962 World's Fair and has since become an iconic symbol of Seattle.

Website: http://www.spaceneedle.com/

Washington State Ferries

Explore Seattle and its surrounding islands with a ferry ride on the Washington State Ferries. This is the largest ferry system in the US, carrying over 24 million passengers annually across Puget Sound and its islands. Enjoy views of the waterfront skyline while sailing to some of Seattle's most popular attractions including Bainbridge Island, Bremerton, and Vashon Island. The unique feature here is that some ferries have outside decks for passengers to enjoy the fresh sea breeze.

Location: 801 Alaskan Way Pier 52, Seattle, WA 98104-1410

Closest City or Town: Seattle, Washington (Located within the city)

How to Get There: From downtown Seattle, head west on Spring Street. Turn right onto Alaskan Way. The ferry terminal is located at Pier 52.

GPS Coordinates 47.6028305° N, 122.3378842° W

Best Time to Visit: The ferry service operates year-round, although it is more pleasant to take a ride during the summer months when the weather is warmer and sunnier for better views.

Pass/Permit/Fees: Fares vary depending on the route. Fares vary per route and tickets can be purchased online or at the ferry terminals.

Did You Know? The Washington State Ferry System is the largest in the US and the third largest in the world by ridership!

Website: https://www.wsdot.wa.gov/ferries/

Museum of Pop Culture

Unleash your inner pop culture enthusiast at the Museum of Pop Culture, a vibrant hub of creativity and innovation located in the heart of Seattle. Showcasing a diverse range of music, film, and television artifacts, the museum offers an immersive journey through the pop culture landscape. Don't miss the unique experience of Sound Lab, where you can try your hand at being a rock star!

Location: 325 5th Ave N Seattle Center, Seattle, WA 98109-4630

Closest City or Town: Seattle

How to Get There: From downtown Seattle, head north on 5th Ave towards Westlake Ave, continue straight onto Broad St, and then turn left onto 5th Ave N. The museum is located within the Seattle Center complex.

GPS Coordinates: 47.6214466° N, 122.3482829° W

Best Time to Visit: The museum is open year-round, with extended hours during the summer months.

Pass/Permit/Fees: Admission fees apply, please visit the website for details.

Did You Know? The museum was founded by Microsoft co-founder Paul Allen in 2000.

Website: http://www.mopop.org/

The Museum of Flight

The Museum of Flight will take you on a tour through the fascinating world of aviation. It is the world's biggest independent aviation and space museum, located in Seattle. Explore the secrets of flying through interactive exhibitions and be amazed by the magnificent collection of aircraft and spacecraft.

Location: 9404 East Marginal Way South, Seattle, WA 98108-4046

Closest City or Town: Seattle

How to Get There: From Seattle downtown, head south on 4th Ave towards Airport Way S, and continue onto E Marginal Way S. The museum is on the right.

GPS Coordinates: 47.517993° N, 122.296384° W

Best Time to Visit: The museum is open year-round, however, summer is the peak season.

Pass/Permit/Fees: Admission fees apply, please visit the website for details.

Did You Know? The museum is home to over 175 aircraft and spacecraft, thousands of artifacts, and millions of rare photographs.

Website: http://www.museumofflight.org/

T-Mobile Park

Experience baseball in a whole new way at the iconic T-Mobile Park. This spectacular arena, which serves as the home of the Seattle Mariners, offers breathtaking vistas of downtown Seattle and Puget Sound. Feel the adrenaline and excitement as you cheer on your favorite team during an incredible game day experience!

Location: 1250 1st Ave S, Seattle, WA 98134-1216

Closest City or Town: Seattle

How to Get There: From downtown Seattle, head south on 4th Ave towards Airport Way S, continue onto E Marginal Way S and then turn left onto 1st Ave S. The stadium will be on the right.

GPS Coordinates: 47.5911209° N, 122.3312259° W

Best Time to Visit: Baseball games run from April through October.

Pass/Permit/Fees: Tickets must be purchased in advance for all events, please visit the website for details.

Did You Know? The building was originally named Safeco Field when it opened in 1999 and was renamed T-Mobile Park in 2019.

Website: https://www.mlb.com/mariners/ballpark

Seattle Aquarium

Journey beneath the waves at the Seattle Aquarium, located at Pier 59 along Elliott Bay's waterfront. Get up close to fascinating sea creatures as you explore the multiple exhibits, and learn about aquatic life in the Pacific Northwest. Don't miss the chance to meet a friendly sea otter up close!

Location: 1483 Alaskan Way Pier 59, Seattle, WA 98101-2015

Closest City or Town: Seattle

How to Get There: From Downtown Seattle, head west on Pike St towards 2nd Ave and then turn left onto Alaskan Way. The aquarium is located at Pier 59.

GPS Coordinates: 47.6073853° N, 122.3421874° W

Best Time to Visit: The aquarium is open year-round, however, summer is the peak season for visitors.

Pass/Permit/Fees: Admission fees apply, please visit the website for details.

Did You Know? The aquarium is home to over 500 species of aquatic life, from invertebrates and fish to mammals and birds.

Website: http://www.seattleaquarium.org/

Kerry Park

Take in breathtaking views of Seattle from Kerry Park, located on Queen Anne Hill. Located just a short drive from downtown, this popular park offers stunning views of the city skyline and Mount Rainier. Don't forget to bring your camera for some picture-perfect memories!

Location: 250 W Highland Dr. Queen Ann Hill, Seattle, WA 98119-3529

Closest City or Town: Seattle

How to Get There: From downtown Seattle, head north on 3rd Ave towards Denny Way and then turn left onto Queen Anne Ave N. Continue onto W Highland Dr and the park will be on the right.

GPS Coordinates: 47.6297851° N, 122.3603506° W

Best Time to Visit: The park is open all year round, however, summer months offer the best views of Seattle and Mt Rainier.

Pass/Permit/Fees: Admission is free of charge.

Did You Know? Kerry Park was originally established as a public park in 1912 and continues to be a popular destination for locals and visitors alike.

Website: https://www.seattle.gov/parks/find/parks/kerry-park

Seattle Great Wheel

Find your sense of wonder and exhilaration at the Seattle Great Wheel, a 175-foot tall Ferris wheel with views of Elliott Bay, Mount Rainier, and the surrounding cityscape. This iconic structure is positioned on Pier 57 overlooking Puget Sound, making it a popular spot for locals and visitors alike! After you ride the wheel, you can explore the Seattle waterfront and nearby attractions such as Aquarium or grab a bite to eat in one of the restaurants.

Location: 1301 Alaskan Way, Seattle, WA 98101-2013

Closest City or Town: Seattle, Washington

How to Get There: Take I-5 north to Exit 164A and follow the signs to the waterfront. Once there, look for Pier 56/57 and you will see The Great Wheel.

GPS Coordinates: 47.605956° N, 122.341148° W

Best Time to Visit: Summer is the best time to visit due to long days with plenty of sunlight!

Pass/Permit/Fees: Entrance fee is $13 per person and is free for children under 2 years old.

Did You Know? The Seattle Great Wheel was the first of its kind on the west coast when it opened in June 2012!

Website: http://seattlegreatwheel.com/

Sky View Observatory

Experience the beauty of Seattle from a unique perspective at Sky View Observatory, located on the 73rd floor of the Columbia Center. Here, visitors can admire 360-degree views of Puget Sound and surrounding mountain ranges, as well as take in the vibrant city skyline from this incredible vantage point! Make sure to come prepared with your camera or binoculars for some truly iconic shots.

Location: 700 4th Ave 73rd floor, Columbia Center, Seattle, WA 98104-7097

Closest City or Town: Seattle, Washington

How to Get There: Take I-5 south to Exit 164A and follow the signs to the waterfront. Once there, look for the Columbia Tower and you will find the Sky View Observatory.

GPS Coordinates: 47.6254283° N, 122.3488931° W

Best Time to Visit: The best time to visit is during sunset for breathtaking views of Seattle's skyline!

Pass/Permit/Fees: The admission fee is $16 per person and is free for children under 4 years old.

Did You Know? Sky View Observatory is the tallest public viewing area in the Pacific Northwest, offering views of up to 150 miles on a clear day!

Website: https://www.skyviewobservatory.com/

Seattle Public Library

Explore one of America's most beautiful libraries at Seattle Public Library in downtown Seattle. Built-in 2004, this glass and steel building houses over 1 million books, as well as many other collections ranging from CDs to DVDs. Visitors can visit the reading rooms for some quiet studying or take part in one of the library's creative programs such as author talks or children's activities.

Location: 1000 4th Ave, Seattle, WA 98104-1109

Closest City or Town: Seattle, Washington

How to Get There: Take I-5 south to Exit 164A and follow the signs to the waterfront. Once there, look for 4th Avenue and you will find Seattle Public Library.

GPS Coordinates: 47.6066827° N, 122.3326622° W

Best Time to Visit: The Library is open year-round!

Pass/Permit/Fees: Admission is free.

Did You Know? Seattle Public Library was the first public library in the United States to offer wireless network access to its patrons!

Website: http://www.spl.org/locations/central-library

Woodland Park Zoo

Experience the wild world of animals up close at Woodland Park Zoo in Seattle. This 92-acre zoo is home to over 300 species, including big cats, primates, and elephants! Visitors can explore the different areas of the zoo such as the Asian Tropical Forest or African Savanna and observe the animals in their natural habitats. The zoo also offers educational programs and behind-the-scenes tours for a more intimate experience.

Location: 5500 Phinney Ave N, Seattle, WA 98103-5897

Closest City or Town: Seattle, Washington

How to Get There: Take I-5 south to Exit 164A and follow the signs to the waterfront. Once there, look for Phinney Avenue North and you will find Woodland Park Zoo.

GPS Coordinates: 47.6686097° N, 122.3543027° W

Best Time to Visit: The best time to visit is during spring or summer when the weather is warm and makes outdoor exploration more enjoyable!

Pass/Permit/Fees: Entrance fee is $17.95 per person and is free for children under 2 years old.

Did You Know? Woodland Park Zoo was ranked one of the top 10 zoos in the United States by TripAdvisor in 2018!

Website: http://www.zoo.org/

Pacific Science Center

Embark on a journey of discovery at the Pacific Science Center in Seattle. With a range of interactive exhibits, it's a great place for kids and adults to learn about science in a fun, engaging way. Don't miss the Tropical Butterfly House, filled with hundreds of beautiful, free-flying butterflies from around the world!

Location: 200 2nd Ave N, Seattle, WA 98109-4895

Closest City or Town: Seattle, Washington

How to Get There: From downtown Seattle, head northwest on 2nd Ave toward Vine St, then turn right onto 2nd Ave N. The Pacific Science Center will be on your right.

GPS Coordinates: 47.6195515° N, 122.3512806° W

Best Time to Visit: The center is open year-round, but visiting on weekdays can help avoid larger crowds.

Pass/Permit/Fees: General admission is $23.95 for adults, $14.95 for children (3-12), and $19.95 for seniors (65+).

Did You Know? The Pacific Science Center started as the United States Science Pavilion during the 1962 World's Fair.

Website: http://www.pacificsciencecenter.org/

Seattle Waterfront

Stroll along the Seattle Waterfront, a bustling, vibrant area filled with restaurants, parks, piers, and stunning views of Puget Sound. The iconic Seattle Great Wheel, a towering Ferris wheel, offers panoramic views of the city. And don't miss the chance to visit Pike Place Market, just a short walk away!

Location: Alaskan Way, Seattle, WA 98101

Closest City or Town: Seattle, Washington

How to Get There: From downtown Seattle, head west on Spring St toward 1st Ave, then turn left onto Alaskan Way. The waterfront will be on your right.

GPS Coordinates: 47.6077692° N, 122.3424489° W

Best Time to Visit: The waterfront is a year-round destination, but it sparkles extra brightly in the summer months.

Pass/Permit/Fees: Entry to the waterfront is free, although certain attractions may charge admission fees.

Did You Know? The Seattle Great Wheel was the tallest Ferris wheel on the West Coast when it opened in 2012.

Website: http://seattlewaterfront.org/

Fremont Troll

Experience a quirky side of Seattle at Fremont Troll, a massive public sculpture lurking beneath the George Washington Memorial Bridge. This whimsical piece of public art, clutching a real Volkswagen Beetle in its hand, offers a unique photo opportunity and has become a beloved symbol of the city's Fremont neighborhood.

Location: North 36th Street, Troll Ave N, Seattle, WA 98103

Closest City or Town: Seattle, Washington

How to Get There: From downtown Seattle, head north on Interstate 5, then take exit 169 toward NE 45th St. Turn right onto N 36th St, and you'll find the troll under the bridge.

GPS Coordinates: 47.6509559° N, 122.3473309° W

Best Time to Visit: The troll is available to visit year-round, day or night. But visiting in daylight offers the best photo opportunities.

Pass/Permit/Fees: Free to visit.

Did You Know? Local artists constructed the Fremont Troll in 1990 in response to a community-wide contest to restore the area under the bridge, which was becoming a dumping place.

Website: http://fremont.com/about/fremonttroll-html

CenturyLink Field

Experience the electrifying energy of CenturyLink Field, home of the Seattle Seahawks and Seattle Sounders. Situated in the heart of Seattle, it provides an awe-inspiring view of the city skyline. Here, you can immerse yourself in the passion of the game, feel the roar of the crowd, and witness live sports at its finest - a truly unique experience!

Location: 800 Occidental Ave S, Seattle, WA 98134-1200

Closest City or Town: Seattle, Washington

How to Get There: Located in the Pioneer Square neighborhood, it is easily accessible from I-5 and I-90. Follow the signs for CenturyLink Field.

GPS Coordinates: 47.5933101° N, 122.3322722° W

Best Time to Visit: During game days for an unforgettable experience.

Pass/Permit/Fees: Varies depending on the event. Visit the website for details.

Did You Know? CenturyLink Field is known for its deafening crowd noise, which often gives the home team an advantage!

Website: http://www.centurylinkfield.com/

Green Lake Park

Green Lake Park, a jewel in the crown of Seattle, offers an idyllic escape in the city! Located in northern Seattle, this park offers a wide array of activities. Whether you enjoy peaceful strolls, brisk jogs, boating, or simply picnicking by the lake, there's something for everyone. The park's unique feature? Its delightful 2.8-mile loop path provides stunning lake views!

Location: 7201 E Green Lake Dr. N, Seattle, WA 98115-5301

Closest City or Town: Seattle, Washington

How to Get There: Take I-5, then exit on NE 71st St and follow signs to Green Lake Park.

GPS Coordinates: 47.6805864° N, 122.3275836° W

Best Time to Visit: Year-round, though spring and summer are the prime times for outdoor activities.

Pass/Permit/Fees: Entry is free.

Did You Know? Green Lake is a glacial lake; its basin was dug 50,000 years ago by the Vashon glacier!

Website:
http://www.cityofseattle.net/parks/parkspaces/greenlak.htm

Alki Beach

Experience the charm of Seattle's coastline at Alki Beach, a vibrant stretch of sand that boasts stunning views of Puget Sound and the Seattle skyline. Enjoy a leisurely stroll, participate in beach volleyball, or simply soak in the scenic beauty. Don't miss the iconic Statue of Liberty, a smaller replica of the famous New York landmark!

Location: Alki Beach, Seattle, Washington 98116

Closest City or Town: Seattle, Washington

How to Get There: From downtown Seattle, head southwest on the West Seattle Bridge. Take the Harbor Ave exit and continue on Harbor Ave SW. Turn right onto Alki Ave SW.

GPS Coordinates: 47.5799° N, 122.4106° W

Best Time to Visit: Summer for beach activities, but the picturesque views are year-round.

Pass/Permit/Fees: Free

Did You Know? Alki Beach was the west coast's first public saltwater bathing beach.

Website: https://www.seattle.gov/parks/allparks/alki-beach-park

Klondike Gold Rush National Historical Park

Transport yourself back to the time of the gold rush at Klondike Gold Rush National Historical Park. Located in the heart of Seattle, this park offers a glimpse into the lives of those who flocked to the region in hopes of striking it rich. Explore exhibits, watch films, and participate in ranger-led programs to experience this fascinating chapter of history.

Location: 319 2nd Ave S, Seattle, WA 98104-2618

Closest City or Town: Seattle, Washington

How to Get There: In downtown Seattle, head south on 2nd Ave. Turn right at S. Main St. and the park will be on your left.

GPS Coordinates: 47.6015° N, 122.3343° W

Best Time to Visit: Open year-round, but summer offers the most programming.

Pass/Permit/Fees: Free

Did You Know? This park is part of a larger international park that commemorates the 1897-1898 gold rush in North America.

Website: http://www.nps.gov/klse/

Gas Works Park

Experience a unique blend of industrial heritage and recreational activities at Gas Works Park, an iconic landmark in Seattle, Washington. This innovative public park, once the site of a gasification plant, now offers green spaces, picnic areas, and panoramic views of downtown Seattle. The park's unique feature is its preserved gasification plant, providing a fascinating glimpse into Seattle's industrial past.

Location: 2101 N Northlake Way, Seattle, WA 98103-9122

Closest City or Town: Seattle, Washington

How to Get There: From I-5 N, take exit 169 toward NE 45th St. Turn right onto 5th Ave NE, then left onto NE 45th St. Make a slight right onto 7th Ave NE and continue onto N Northlake Way to the park.

GPS Coordinates: 47.6462405° N, 122.3336973° W

Best Time to Visit: Open year-round, but the summer months offer the best opportunities to enjoy the park's outdoor activities.

Pass/Permit/Fees: Admission to the park is free and no permits are required.

Did You Know? In addition to its stunning views, Gas Works Park also features a children's play barn formed from the remains of an old coal gasification plant.

Website: http://www.ci.seattle.wa.us/parks/home.htm

Discovery Park

Uncover the wild heart of Seattle at Discovery Park, the city's largest green space with breathtaking views of Puget Sound and the Cascade Mountains. This park offers a range of experiences, from hiking and birdwatching to beachcombing and picnicking on its 534 acres.

Location: 3801 Discovery Park Blvd, Seattle, WA 98199-1029

Closest City or Town: Seattle, Washington

How to Get There: From the city center, take Elliot Ave W and turn left onto W Mercer St. Merge onto 15th Ave W and take the exit toward Emerson St. Turn left onto Gilman Ave W and continue onto Discovery Park Blvd.

GPS Coordinates: 47.661979° N, 122.4357206° W

Best Time to Visit: Year-round, but spring and summer offer the best weather for outdoor activities.

Pass/Permit/Fees: The park is free to enter.

Did You Know? The park is home to more than 270 species of birds.

Website: http://www.cityofseattle.net/parks/Environment/discovparkindex.htm

Museum of History & Industry

Unearth the rich history of the Emerald City at the Museum of History & Industry. Located at Lake Union Park in Seattle, Washington, this museum showcases a multitude of artifacts that narrate the city's past. Immerse yourself in stories of innovation, transformation, and diversity that define Seattle's unique trajectory.

Location: 860 Terry Ave N, Seattle, WA 98109-4330

Closest City or Town: Seattle, Washington

How to Get There: From downtown Seattle, head northeast on Virginia St towards 5th Ave, then turn left onto Boren Ave. Continue onto Fairview Ave, then onto Terry Ave to reach the museum.

GPS Coordinates: 47.6276176° N, 122.3365807° W

Best Time to Visit: All year round

Pass/Permit/Fees: Please refer to their website for current fees

Did You Know? MOHAI is home to an impressive collection of more than four million artifacts!

Website: http://mohai.org/

Smith Tower Visitor Experience

Reach for the sky at the Smith Tower Visitor Experience, one of Seattle's oldest skyscrapers. Nestled in the heart of the city, the building's 35th-floor observatory offers panoramic views that will leave you breathless. A visit to the Prohibition-themed speakeasy adds an extra dash of charm to the experience.

Location: 500 2nd Ave, Seattle, WA 98104-2336

Closest City or Town: Seattle, Washington

How to Get There: From Pioneer Square, walk north on 1st Ave. Turn right onto Cherry St, then left onto 2nd Ave, and you'll find Smith Tower on your right.

GPS Coordinates: 47.6018382° N, 122.3318427° W

Best Time to Visit: All year, but summer offers the clearest views

Pass/Permit/Fees: Visit their website for current pricing

Did You Know? When it opened in 1914, Smith Tower was the tallest office building outside New York City!

Website: http://smithtower.com/

Washington Park Arboretum

Experience the wonders of botanical diversity at Washington Park Arboretum, a joint project of the University of Washington and the city of Seattle. With over 230 acres of gardens, this green sanctuary showcases a vast range of plant species, making it an ideal place for a peaceful stroll or a picnic amidst nature.

Location: 2300 Arboretum Dr. E, Seattle, WA 98195-8010

Closest City or Town: Seattle, Washington

How to Get There: Located in the heart of the city, the arboretum is easily accessible from all major routes in Seattle.

GPS Coordinates: 47.6397846° N, 122.294488° W

Best Time to Visit: Spring, when the cherry blossoms are in bloom.

Pass/Permit/Fees: Free. No passes or fees are required.

Did You Know? The arboretum houses one of the most comprehensive collections of maple trees in the world.

Website: http://depts.washington.edu/uwbg/gardens/wpa.shtml

Pike Place Fish Market

Experience the energy and excitement of Pike Place Fish Market, a renowned landmark in the vibrant city of Seattle. Revel in the bustling atmosphere as the market's famous fishmongers showcase their skill and flair, hurling fish through the air with remarkable precision!

Location: 86 Pike St, Seattle, WA 98101-2025

Closest City or Town: Seattle, Washington

How to Get There: Pike Place Market is located in downtown Seattle, close to the waterfront, and is easily accessible by foot, bike, bus, or car.

GPS Coordinates: 47.6088877° N, 122.3405181° W

Best Time to Visit: The market is open year-round, but the fish-tossing spectacle is best in the mornings.

Pass/Permit/Fees: No entry fee.

Did You Know? The fish-tossing tradition at Pike Place Fish Market began as a practical way to avoid walking back and forth to retrieve fish.

Website: http://www.pikeplacefish.com/

Bill & Melinda Gates Foundation Discovery Center

Unleash your inner philanthropist at the Bill & Melinda Gates Foundation Discovery Center located in Seattle. This interactive exhibition provides a deep dive into the world-changing work of the foundation. Engage in interactive exhibits, immersive storytelling, and global conversations that will inspire and challenge you to create a better world.

Location: 440 5th Ave N, Seattle, WA 98109-4631

Closest City or Town: Seattle, Washington

How to Get There: From downtown Seattle, head north on 5th Avenue until you reach the Discovery Center just beyond Broad Street.

GPS Coordinates: 47.6226034° N, 122.3467906° W

Best Time to Visit: All year round

Pass/Permit/Fees: Free admission

Did You Know? The Discovery Center has a dedicated Youth Ambassadors Program which enables young people to learn about global issues and philanthropy.

Website: http://www.discovergates.org/

Bruce Lee Grave Site

Pay your respects to the martial arts legend, Bruce Lee, at his gravesite located in the scenic Lake View Cemetery in Seattle. This peaceful location is a must-visit for fans wanting to honor and remember the star who was taken too soon.

Location: 1554 15th Ave E, Seattle, WA 98112-2805

Closest City or Town: Seattle, Washington

How to Get There: From downtown Seattle, head east on Pike St. Turn left onto 15th Ave E, and the cemetery will be on your left.

GPS Coordinates: 47.6339171° N, 122.3121751° W

Best Time to Visit: The site is open year-round, but be sure to check the cemetery's visiting hours.

Pass/Permit/Fees: There is no entry fee.

Did You Know? Bruce Lee's son, Brandon Lee, is buried next to him.

Website: http://www.seattle.gov/html/visitor/graves.htm

Benaroya Hall

Located in the heart of downtown Seattle, Benaroya Hall is the crown jewel of the city's cultural scene. The home of the Seattle Symphony, the hall boasts world-class acoustics and a breathtaking glass art installation in its grand lobby.

Location: 200 University St, Seattle, WA 98101, United States

Closest City or Town: Seattle, Washington

How to Get There: Benaroya Hall is located on the corner of Third Avenue and University Street in downtown Seattle. It is easily accessible by public transit or by car with a variety of nearby parking options.

GPS Coordinates: 47.608073° N, 122.3368964° W

Best Time to Visit: Anytime a performance aligns with your schedule.

Pass/Permit/Fees: Ticket prices vary based on performance. Please visit their website for more details.

Did You Know? Benaroya Hall is named after Jack and Rebecca Benaroya, whose generous donation made the construction of this architectural marvel possible.

Website: http://www.benaroyahall.org/

Kubota Garden

Experience the serene beauty of Kubota Garden, a beautiful 20-acre landscape that combines Japanese garden ideals with native Northwest species. The garden is a masterpiece of horticulture that offers a unique experience in every season.

Location: 9817 55th Ave S, Seattle, WA 98118-5710

Closest City or Town: Seattle, Washington

How to Get There: From I-5, take the Swift Ave exit (exit 161). Go north on Swift Ave, then east on S Graham St, which becomes 55th Ave S. The garden is on the left.

GPS Coordinates: 47.5128317° N, 122.2650264° W

Best Time to Visit: Spring for cherry blossoms, Fall for autumn colors

Pass/Permit/Fees: Entry to the garden is free.

Did You Know? The garden was created by Japanese emigrant Fujitaro Kubota in 1927.

Website: http://www.kubotagarden.org/

5th Avenue Theatre

Immerse yourself in the magic of live performances at the 5th Avenue Theatre, a historic gem located in the heart of Seattle, Washington. Hosting a variety of musicals, plays, and concerts, this theatre guarantees an unforgettable night out!

Location: 1308 5th Ave, Seattle, WA 98101-2602

Closest City or Town: Seattle, Washington

How to Get There: Located in downtown Seattle, the theatre is easily accessible by public transit, car, or on foot.

GPS Coordinates: 47.6093875° N, 122.3338379° W

Best Time to Visit: Year-round, check their calendar for show schedules.

Pass/Permit/Fees: Ticket prices vary depending on the show.

Did You Know? The theatre was built in 1926 and is one of the nation's leading musical theater companies.

Website: http://www.5thavenue.org/

Volunteer Park Conservatory

Step into a lush, tropical oasis at the Volunteer Park Conservatory, a beautiful greenhouse located in Seattle, Washington. Home to a diverse collection of plants from around the world, this is a must-visit for nature lovers!

Location: 1402 E Galer St, Seattle, WA 98112-2843

Closest City or Town: Seattle, Washington

How to Get There: Located in the Capitol Hill neighborhood of Seattle, the conservatory is easily accessible by public transit, car, or on foot.

GPS Coordinates: 47.6321127° N, 122.3157383° W

Best Time to Visit: Year-round, but the conservatory is particularly beautiful in the spring when many plants are in bloom.

Pass/Permit/Fees: Entry is $4 for adults, $2 for youth, and free for children 12 and under.

Did You Know? The conservatory is over 100 years old and is home to over 600 different plant species.

Website: http://www.ci.seattle.wa.us/parks/home.htm

Seattle Japanese Garden

Escape the hustle-bustle of the city and surrender to the tranquillity of the Seattle Japanese Garden. Located in the heart of Seattle, this serene oasis recreates the allure of traditional Japanese gardens and offers a unique experience of meditation and contemplation.

Location: 1075 Lake Washington Blvd E, Seattle, WA 98112-3755

Closest City or Town: Seattle, Washington

How to Get There: From I-5, take exit 168B to merge onto WA-520 E towards Bellevue/Kirkland. Take the Montlake Blvd exit, then continue onto 24th Ave E. Turn right onto E Lynn St, then continue onto Lake Washington Blvd E.

GPS Coordinates: 47.6290032° N, 122.2963693° W

Best Time to Visit: Spring and Fall when the garden is ablaze with seasonal colors.

Pass/Permit/Fees: Entrance fees apply, please check their website for more details.

Did You Know? The Seattle Japanese Garden is one of North America's oldest Japanese gardens and is regarded as one of the most authentic outside of Japan.

Website: http://www.seattlejapanesegarden.org/

Lake Union

Immerse yourself in the tranquility of Lake Union. Located in the heart of Seattle, this urban oasis offers a multitude of activities, from sailing and kayaking to dining at lakeside restaurants. Soak in the stunning skyline views and watch seaplanes take off and land – a unique Lake Union spectacle.

Location: 2349 Fairview Ave E, Seattle, WA 98102, United States

Closest City or Town: Seattle, Washington

How to Get There: From downtown Seattle, head north on Fairview Ave E, and the lake will be on your right.

GPS Coordinates: 47.6413287° N, 122.330442° W

Best Time to Visit: Summer months when water activities are in full swing.

Pass/Permit/Fees: Free to visit, but fees may apply for specific activities or rentals.

Did You Know? Lake Union is known as the "Center of Seattle" due to its central location.

Website: http://www.visitseattle.org/neighborhoods/south-lake-union

Lake Washington

Experience Seattle's largest lake, Lake Washington. This natural marvel separates the city of Seattle from the Eastside. It is a popular spot for boating, watersports, and picnicking on the shores, with splendid views of Mount Rainier in the distance.

Location: Lake Washington, Seattle, Washington WA

Closest City or Town: Seattle, Washington

How to Get There: Driving from downtown Seattle, head east on WA-520. You'll see the lake on both sides of the highway.

GPS Coordinates: 47.6215474° N, 122.255756° W

Best Time to Visit: Summer is the best time for water activities, though the lake is beautiful all year round.

Pass/Permit/Fees: Free to visit, but fees may apply for boat rentals and other activities.

Did You Know? Lake Washington is the state of Washington's second-largest natural lake.

Website: http://www.choicehotels.com/washington/renton/econo-lodge-hotels/wa148

Columbia Center

Soar high above Seattle at the Columbia Center's Sky View Observatory! Located in downtown Seattle, Columbia Center is the city's tallest skyscraper, providing unrivaled views of the Emerald City's skyline from its 73rd floor.

Location: 701 5th Ave Ste 4000, Seattle, WA 98104-7072

Closest City or Town: Seattle, WA

How to Get There: Columbia Center is located in the heart of downtown Seattle. It is easily accessible via public transit, including buses and the Link light rail.

GPS Coordinates: 47.6048152° N, 122.3305677° W

Best Time to Visit: Open year-round, but clear days provide the best views.

Pass/Permit/Fees: There are entrance fees to the Sky View Observatory. Check the website for the current rates.

Did You Know? The Sky View Observatory at Columbia Center is the highest public viewing area west of the Mississippi.

Website: http://columbiacenterseattle.com/

Wing Luke Museum of the Asian-Pacific American Experience

Explore the rich history and culture of Asian Pacific Americans at the Wing Luke Museum in Seattle's vibrant International District. The museum, the only pan-Asian Pacific American community-based museum in the U.S., is housed in a historic building that combines traditional Asian aesthetics with contemporary design.

Location: 719 S King St, Seattle, WA 98104-3035

Closest City or Town: Seattle, WA

How to Get There: The museum is located in the Chinatown-International District, which is easily accessible by public transit.

GPS Coordinates: 47.5981368° N, 122.3228286° W

Best Time to Visit: The museum is open year-round, but check the website for any changes in the operating hours.

Pass/Permit/Fees: Admission fees apply. Please visit the museum's website for details.

Did You Know? Not only does the museum feature rotating exhibits, but it's also home to preserved historic hotel rooms that offer a glimpse into Seattle's past.

Website: http://wingluke.org/

Hiram M. Chittenden Locks

Witness the impressive feat of engineering at the Hiram M. Chittenden Locks, also known as the Ballard Locks, a must-visit destination in Seattle, Washington. Observe seagoing vessels of all kinds navigating the locks, a unique blend of maritime tradition and innovative technology. Don't miss a chance to visit the adjacent fish ladder, particularly during the salmon migration season.

Location: 3015 NW 54th St, Seattle, WA 98107-4213

Closest City or Town: Seattle, Washington

How to Get There: From Seattle, follow Elliott Ave W and 15th Ave W to NW Market St in Ballard. Continue on NW Market St to your destination.

GPS Coordinates: 47.6666738° N, 122.3981239° W

Best Time to Visit: Year-round, but the fish ladder is most active from June to September.

Pass/Permit/Fees: Free entry.

Did You Know? The locks are the busiest in the nation, moving more boat traffic than any other U.S. lock system.

Website: http://ballardlocks.org/

Golden Gardens Park

Escape the city's hustle and bustle at Golden Gardens Park, a beautiful beachfront park located in Ballard, a neighborhood in Seattle. Enjoy the stunning views of Puget Sound and the Olympic Mountains, have a picnic, play beach volleyball, or explore the forest trails. When the sun sets, gather around a bonfire for a cozy end to the day.

Location: 8499 Seaview Place NW, Seattle, WA 98117

Closest City or Town: Seattle, Washington

How to Get There: From downtown Seattle, take 15th Ave NW and continue to NW 85th St. Take a right on 32nd Ave NW to get to the park.

GPS Coordinates: 47.6897645° N, 122.4022432° W

Best Time to Visit: Summer months for beach activities and year-round for forest trails

Pass/Permit/Fees: Free entrance. Fire pits are first-come-first-serve.

Did You Know? Golden Gardens Park offers one of the few sandy beaches along Seattle's Puget Sound shoreline.

Website:
http://www.cityofseattle.net/parks/parkspaces/Golden.htm

Waterfall Garden Park

Experience an urban oasis in the bustling city of Seattle at the Waterfall Garden Park. Nestled between skyscrapers, this hidden park offers a respite from city life with its 22-foot waterfall creating a peaceful ambiance. It's the perfect spot to enjoy a quiet lunch, meditate, or simply unwind amid the sounds of the cascading waterfall.

Location: 219 2nd Ave S, Seattle, WA 98104-2601

Closest City or Town: Seattle, Washington

How to Get There: Located in the Pioneer Square neighborhood of Seattle, the park is easily accessible by public transportation.

GPS Coordinates: 47.6002312° N, 122.3320588° W

Best Time to Visit: Open year-round, ideally visited during the spring and summer months.

Pass/Permit/Fees: The park is free to visit.

Did You Know? This park was built in 1978 on the site of United Parcel Service's first office.

Website: http://www.pioneersquare.org/experiences/waterfall-garden-park

Amazon Spheres

Explore the heart of Seattle through a unique botanical journey at the Amazon Spheres. These glass domes house a lush collection of exotic plants, offering a tranquil respite from urban life. Stroll through the various gardens, relax in the seating areas, or grab a coffee at the shop inside.

Location: 2101 7th Ave, Seattle, WA 98121-5114

Closest City or Town: Seattle, Washington

How to Get There: The spheres are located in downtown Seattle on 7th Avenue, between Lenora and Blanchard Streets.

GPS Coordinates: 47.6158195° N, 122.3391805° W

Best Time to Visit: Open year-round, but visitor access is restricted to Amazon employees outside public visiting hours.

Pass/Permit/Fees: Entry is free, but a reservation is required for public visiting hours.

Did You Know? The Amazon Spheres house more than 40,000 plants from 50 different countries.

Website: http://www.seattlespheres.com/

The Center for Wooden Boats

Unleash your inner sailor at The Center for Wooden Boats, located right in the heart of Seattle, Washington. This floating museum is a unique tribute to maritime history and a venue for hands-on learning. Visitors can create their own adventures by renting vintage vessels or taking classes in boat building and sailing.

Location: 1010 Valley St, Seattle, WA 98109-4444

Closest City or Town: Seattle, Washington

How to Get There: From downtown Seattle, head southwest on Madison St toward 4th Ave. Turn right onto Alaskan Way. Turn left onto Valley St.

GPS Coordinates: 47.6264927° N, 122.3357475° W

Best Time to Visit: Open all year round with different activities each season.

Pass/Permit/Fees: Entry to the center is free. Fees apply for boat rentals and classes.

Did You Know? The Center for Wooden Boats has one of the largest collections of vintage boats that visitors can rent and explore on their own.

Website: http://cwb.org/locations/south-lake-union/

SEQUIM

Olympic Game Farm

Connect with nature in a unique way at the Olympic Game Farm, a family-friendly destination in Sequim, Washington. From the comfort of your own vehicle, you can observe a variety of wildlife in a free-ranging environment, creating a truly memorable experience.

Location: 1423 Ward Rd, Sequim, WA 98382-7838

Closest City or Town: Sequim, Washington

How to Get There: From US-101, take the Carlsborg Rd exit and follow signs to Olympic Game Farm.

GPS Coordinates: 48.1351935° N, 123.1468624° W

Best Time to Visit: The farm is open year-round, but animal sightings are more frequent during the warmer months.

Pass/Permit/Fees: Admission fees apply, check the website for current prices.

Did You Know? The Olympic Game Farm was originally a holding facility for Walt Disney Studios' nature films.

Website: http://www.olygamefarm.com/

Dungeness National Wildlife Refuge

Dungeness National Wildlife Refuge, located in Sequim, Washington, is a paradise for nature lovers. The refuge is home to over 250 species of birds and offers a wide range of activities such as birdwatching, hiking, and photography. Walk along the serene coastal trails and embrace the tranquility of this natural haven.

Location: 554 Voice of America Rd, Sequim, WA 98382-9537

Closest City or Town: Sequim, Washington

How to Get There: From Sequim, take US-101 E and turn right onto Kitchen-Dick Rd. Turn right again onto Lotzgesell Rd and follow signs to the Wildlife Refuge.

GPS Coordinates: 48.1411526° N, 123.1909006° W

Best Time to Visit: Spring and Fall are the best times to visit for birdwatching.

Pass/Permit/Fees: A small entry fee is required. Check their website for more details.

Did You Know? The Dungeness Spit, the longest natural sand spit in the United States, is located within the refuge!

Website: http://www.dungeness.com/refuge/

Purple Haze Lavender Farm

Experience the tranquil beauty of Purple Haze Lavender Farm, a serene retreat located in Sequim, Washington. You may walk through aromatic lavender fields, buy handcrafted lavender goods, and even try lavender ice cream! The farm's beautiful scenery and relaxing environment make it a one-of-a-kind and unforgettable location.

Location: 180 Bell Bottom Rd, Sequim, WA 98382-9005

Closest City or Town: Sequim, Washington

How to Get There: From Sequim, take W Washington St and turn onto N 5th Ave. Follow the road until you reach Bell Bottom Rd, and then follow the signs to Purple Haze Lavender Farm.

GPS Coordinates: 48.0738229° N, 123.0665081° W

Best Time to Visit: Visit in July for the annual Lavender Festival when the fields are in full bloom.

Pass/Permit/Fees: Entry to the farm is free, but there may be a fee for certain activities.

Did You Know? Sequim's Mediterranean-like climate makes it an ideal location for lavender cultivation.

Website: http://www.purplehazelavender.com/

B&B Family Farm

Immerse yourself in the charming rural beauty of the B&B Family Farm, located in the idyllic town of Sequim, Washington. Known for its lavender fields and picturesque landscapes, the farm offers a unique experience for visitors. You can participate in the lavender harvest, see how lavender oil is distilled, and purchase high-quality lavender products directly from the farm.

Location: 5883 Old Olympic Hwy, Sequim, WA 98382-7451

Closest City or Town: Sequim, Washington

How to Get There: From Sequim, take the Old Olympic Highway east for about 5 miles. The farm is on your right.

GPS Coordinates: 48.105658° N, 123.181278° W

Best Time to Visit: July and August during lavender blooming season.

Pass/Permit/Fees: Free entry, charges for certain activities and purchases.

Did You Know? B&B Family Farm is one of the few farms that allows you to participate in the harvest and distillation process.

Website: http://bbfamilyfarm.com/

SNOQUALMIE

Snoqualmie Falls

Experience the breathtaking beauty of Snoqualmie Falls, a 268-foot waterfall located in Snoqualmie, Washington. This natural wonder offers fantastic views from both the top and the bottom of the falls, and the two-acre park area is perfect for picnics. Don't miss the short trail to the lower observation deck, where you can truly experience the power and beauty of the falls.

Location: 6501 Railroad Ave SE, Snoqualmie, WA 98065-9687

Closest City or Town: Snoqualmie, Washington

How to Get There: From Snoqualmie, head southeast on Railroad Ave SE toward SE Northern St. The falls will be on your left.

GPS Coordinates: 47.5420817° N, 121.8365133° W

Best Time to Visit: The falls are most spectacular during the rainy season in late fall and winter.

Pass/Permit/Fees: The park is free to visit and open to the public.

Did You Know? The name 'Snoqualmie' comes from the Snoqualmie people, a local Native American tribe who consider the falls to be a place of spiritual power.

Website: http://www.snoqualmiefalls.com/

SPOKANE

Riverfront Park

Immerse yourself in the natural beauty of Spokane at Riverfront Park, located in the heart of downtown. This urban oasis offers a variety of outdoor activities, including walking paths, picnic areas, and a stunning view of Spokane Falls. Don't forget to take a ride on the iconic Spokane Falls Skyride for an unforgettable aerial view of the falls.

Location: 507 N Howard St, Spokane, WA 99201-0811

Closest City or Town: Spokane, Washington

How to Get There: From downtown Spokane, follow W Riverside Ave and turn right onto N Howard St. The park will be on your left.

GPS Coordinates: 47.6606651° N, 117.4203235° W

Best Time to Visit: The park is open year-round, but spring and fall are particularly beautiful due to the blossoming flowers and autumn leaves.

Pass/Permit/Fees: Entry to the park is free, but fees are charged for certain activities and attractions.

Did You Know? Riverfront Park was the site for World's Fair 1974, a special event themed on environmental conservation.

Website: http://riverfrontspokane.org/

Manito Park

Immerse yourself in the natural beauty of Manito Park, a horticultural wonderland located in Spokane, Washington. This enchanting park boasts five unique gardens, a conservatory filled with tropical plants, and a serene duck pond.

Location: 1702 S. Grand Blvd., Spokane, WA 99203

Closest City or Town: Spokane, Washington

How to Get There: From downtown Spokane, head south on S. Grand Blvd. The park will be on the right-hand side.

GPS Coordinates: 47.6364762° N, 117.4124515° W

Best Time to Visit: The park is open year-round, but spring is the best time to see the flowers in full bloom.

Pass/Permit/Fees: Free to visit.

Did You Know? Manito Park, established in 1904, covers 90 acres, and its name is derived from the Algonquin word 'Manitou' which means 'spirit'.

Website: http://my.spokanecity.org/parks/major/manito/

Spokane Falls

Experience the roaring power of nature at Spokane Falls, a natural beauty set right in the heart of downtown Spokane. Witness the spectacular waterfall on a gondola skylift ride, or take a leisurely stroll around Riverfront Park. The falls, a sacred site for the Spokane Tribe, have provided sustenance and spiritual inspiration for centuries.

Location: Monroe Street Bridge, 218 N Monroe St, Spokane, WA 99201, United States

Closest City or Town: Spokane, Washington

How to Get There: Located in the heart of downtown Spokane, it's easily accessible by foot, bike, or car. If driving, parking is available at the City Parking Garage on North Post Street.

GPS Coordinates: 47.6605791° N, 117.4266527° W

Best Time to Visit: The best time to visit is May through September when temperatures are warm and there are no snowmelt runoffs from surrounding mountains.

Pass/Permit/Fees: No entrance fees.

Did You Know? The waterfall was a center of culture and commerce for the Spokane Tribe long before white settlers arrived in the area.

Website: https://spokanehistorical.org/items/show/507

Centennial Trail

Explore the wonders of Spokane, Washington on the Centennial Trail, a scenic 37-mile pathway that runs along the Spokane River. Located at 404 N Havana Street in Spokane, this trail is a great spot for running, walking, cycling, or rollerblading.

Location: 404 N Havana Street Spokane, WA 99202

Closest City or Town: Spokane, Washington

How to Get There: From downtown Spokane, take N Havana Street north until you reach the beginning of the trail.

GPS Coordinates: 47.6623196° N, 117.3464927° W

Best Time to Visit: The Centennial Trail is open year-round and offers visitors a chance to explore Spokane's vibrant natural surroundings all year long.

Pass/Permit/Fees: Entrance is free.

Did You Know? The Centennial Trail was first constructed in the late 1980s and now stretches from Spokane to Nine Mile Falls!

Website: http://www.spokanecentennialtrail.org/

Green Bluff

Immerse yourself in the rural charm of Green Bluff, an agricultural heartland nestled up in the hills of Mead, Washington. The area, famed for its U-pick orchards and breweries, offers a fun-filled day for families and foodies alike. Don't miss the opportunity to taste the freshest produce directly from the trees and sip on some locally brewed cider!

Location: 9910 E Day Mt Spokane Rd, Mead, WA 99021

Closest City or Town: Spokane, WA

How to Get There: From Spokane, follow U.S. Route 2 north and take Exit 289 towards Mt. Spokane. Continue on E. Day Mt. Spokane Rd to reach Green Bluff.

GPS Coordinates: 47.8273419° N, 117.2713826° W

Best Time to Visit: Harvest season between September and October is the best time to visit.

Pass/Permit/Fees: No entry fee, cost depends on the produce you pick.

Did You Know? The Green Bluff Growers' Association, the local farming community, hosts annual fruit festivals throughout the harvest season.

Website: http://www.mrskalinsbarn.com/

Martin Woldson Theater at the Fox

Step into the wonder of the performing arts at the Martin Woldson Theater at the Fox, a historic venue in Spokane, Washington. This art deco-style building hosts a variety of performances, from classical music concerts to contemporary dance shows. The theater's stunning architecture, complete with meticulously restored murals and fixtures, makes it a unique destination for culture lovers.

Location: 1001 W Sprague Ave, Spokane, WA 99201-4016

Closest City or Town: Spokane, Washington

How to Get There: From downtown Spokane, head south on Monroe Street until you reach W Sprague Avenue. The theater is located on the corner of Monroe Street and W Sprague Avenue.

GPS Coordinates: 47.6568613° N, 117.4270812° W

Best Time to Visit: The theater has events throughout the year, but the best time to visit will depend on the performance schedule.

Pass/Permit/Fees: Ticket prices depend on the performance, but discounts are available for students and seniors.

Did You Know? The Martin Woldson Theater at the Fox is one of only two art deco-style theaters in the United States.

Website: http://www.foxtheaterspokane.com/

TACOMA

Museum of Glass

Discover the enchantment of glass artistry at the Museum of Glass, a prominent cultural landmark in Tacoma, Washington. From witnessing real-time glassblowing to admiring stunning exhibits, the museum offers a unique exploration of this delicate art form.

Location: 1801 Dock St, Tacoma, WA 98402-3217

Closest City or Town: Tacoma, Washington

How to Get There: The museum is located in downtown Tacoma, easily accessible from I-5 and I-705. Follow signs for City Center and Dock Street.

GPS Coordinates: 47.2458849° N, 122.4341104° W

Best Time to Visit: Anytime during the year as indoor exhibits are climate-controlled.

Pass/Permit/Fees: Standard adult admission is $17, with discounts available for seniors, students, and the military.

Did You Know? The museum is home to the world's largest conical cone-shaped studio for glassblowing!

Website: http://www.museumofglass.org/

Point Defiance Park

Immerse yourself in the stunning natural beauty of Point Defiance Park, a verdant oasis in Tacoma, Washington. Offering a plethora of recreational activities including hiking, boating, and wildlife watching, it's a haven for nature enthusiasts and adventure seekers alike.

Location: 5400 N Pearl St, Tacoma, WA 98407-3224

Closest City or Town: Tacoma, Washington

How to Get There: The park is located in North Tacoma, directly accessible from N Pearl Street.

GPS Coordinates: 47.3040545° N, 122.5177208° W

Best Time to Visit: The park is open year-round, but the spring and summer months offer the best opportunities for outdoor activities.

Pass/Permit/Fees: No entrance fee is required.

Did You Know? The park is home to a century-old pagoda, originally built as a streetcar waiting room!

Website: http://www.metroparkstacoma.org/point-defiance-park

LeMay - America's Car Museum

Rev your engines and head over to LeMay - America's Car Museum, a must-visit destination for automobile enthusiasts. Situated in the vibrant city of Tacoma, Washington, the museum showcases the evolution of automobiles with an impressive collection of over 350 classic cars. Take a journey back in time as you explore exhibits featuring vintage models, and don't miss the unique opportunity to view some rare gems up close!

Location: 2702 E D St, Tacoma, WA 98421-1200

Closest City or Town: Tacoma, Washington

How to Get There: From I-705 S, take the exit toward City Center. Merge onto A St and then turn left onto E 26th St. Turn right onto E D St and you will see the museum.

GPS Coordinates: 47.2363233° N, 122.4304617° W

Best Time to Visit: Open year-round. Check their website for any seasonal closures.

Pass/Permit/Fees: Please check the museum's website for the most accurate admission fees.

Did You Know? The museum is named after Harold LeMay, who once held the Guinness World Record for the largest private car collection.

Website: http://www.americascarmuseum.org/

Point Defiance Zoo & Aquarium

Discover a world of wildlife at Point Defiance Zoo & Aquarium, nestled in the heart of Tacoma, Washington. This family-friendly destination offers a unique blend of marine and terrestrial biodiversity, with exhibits featuring both local and exotic species. Marvel at the underwater wonders in the aquarium, or get up close with the fascinating creatures of the zoo - there's never a dull moment here!

Location: 5400 N Pearl St, Tacoma, WA 98407-3224

Closest City or Town: Tacoma, Washington

How to Get There: From I-5 S, take exit 133 for I-705 N toward City Center. Continue onto Schuster Pkwy and keep right to stay on N Pearl St. Follow N Pearl St to the park.

GPS Coordinates: 47.3040545° N, 122.5177208° W

Best Time to Visit: While open year-round, spring and summer offer more outdoor experiences and events.

Pass/Permit/Fees: Admission fees vary. Please visit their website for the most accurate pricing.

Did You Know? The zoo houses the only combined zoo and aquarium in the Pacific Northwest, making it a unique destination for wildlife lovers.

Website: http://www.pdza.org/

Chihuly Bridge of Glass

Immerse yourself in the mesmerizing display of art at the Chihuly Bridge of Glass in Tacoma. This 500-foot pedestrian overpass is adorned with vibrant glass sculptures designed by world-renowned artist Dale Chihuly. The bridge provides a stunning, colorful gateway to the Museum of Glass, making it a must-visit attraction!

Location: Bridge of Glass, Tacoma, WA 98402

Closest City or Town: Tacoma, Washington

How to Get There: From I-5, take exit 133 for I-705 toward City Center, then take the exit toward S 21st St and turn left onto Dock St until you reach the bridge.

GPS Coordinates: 47.2456664° N, 122.4345766° W

Best Time to Visit: Daytime for the best light reflection on the glass

Pass/Permit/Fees: Free admission

Did You Know? The bridge showcases three distinct installations by Chihuly: The Seaform Pavilion, the Crystal Towers, and the Venetian Wall.

Website: http://museumofglass.org/outdoor-art/chihuly-bridge-of-glass

Tacoma Art Museum

Immerse yourself in the Tacoma Art Museum, located in the heart of Tacoma, Washington. The museum showcases an impressive collection of art that reflects the Pacific Northwest's rich cultural heritage. Highlighting both contemporary and historical works, the museum offers a transformative experience for art lovers.

Location: 1701 Pacific Ave, Tacoma, WA 98402-3214

Closest City or Town: Tacoma, Washington

How to Get There: From Downtown Tacoma, head south on Pacific Ave until you reach the museum.

GPS Coordinates: 47.2477029° N, 122.436428° W

Best Time to Visit: All year round, but check the museum's website for specific exhibition dates.

Pass/Permit/Fees: Adult admission is $18, with discounts available for students, seniors, and the military. Children 5 and under are free.

Did You Know? Tacoma Art Museum is known for its collection of works by glass artist Dale Chihuly, a Tacoma native.

Website: http://www.tacomaartmuseum.org/

5 Mile Drive & Trails

Embark on a journey through nature at 5 Mile Drive and Trails in Tacoma, Washington. Spanning through Point Defiance Park, the trail offers breathtaking views of the Tacoma Narrows and Vashon Island. Whether you decide to drive, bike, or walk, you can immerse yourself in the area's diverse flora and fauna.

Location: 5400 N Pearl St, Tacoma, WA 98407-3224

Closest City or Town: Tacoma, Washington

How to Get There: From Downtown Tacoma, head north on N Pearl St until you reach the entrance of Point Defiance Park.

GPS Coordinates: 47.3040545° N, 122.5177208° W

Best Time to Visit: The trails can be enjoyed year-round, but spring and fall offer the most scenic views.

Pass/Permit/Fees: The park is free to visit.

Did You Know? Point Defiance Park is one of the largest urban parks in the United States.

Website: http://www.metroparkstacoma.org/five-mile-drive

Washington State History Museum

Step back in time at the Washington State History Museum, located in Tacoma. The museum allows the exploration of Washington's heritage through interactive exhibits, dramatic artifacts, and exciting stories. It's an educational, engaging, and thoroughly enjoyable experience for visitors of all ages.

Location: 1911 Pacific Ave, Tacoma, WA 98402-3109

Closest City or Town: Tacoma, Washington

How to Get There: The museum is located in downtown Tacoma, easily accessible via I-5 and I-705.

GPS Coordinates: 47.2447903° N, 122.4359546° W

Best Time to Visit: All year round.

Pass/Permit/Fees: Entrance fees are applicable. Please visit their website for details.

Did You Know? The museum houses more than 7 million unique items relating to Washington State's history.

Website: http://www.washingtonhistory.org/wshm/

TUMWATER

Tumwater Falls Park

Discover the natural beauty of Tumwater Falls Park, a hidden gem nestled in Tumwater, Washington. This park, known for its cascading waterfall, offers a scenic walk along the Deschutes River with interpretive signs about the area's history. The roar of the falls, the lush greenery, and the occasional sighting of salmon make it a must-visit.

Location: 110 Deschutes Way SW, Tumwater, WA 98501-4072

Closest City or Town: Olympia, Washington

How to Get There: From Olympia, head south on I-5, take exit 103 for Deschutes Way and follow the signs to Tumwater Falls Park.

GPS Coordinates: 47.0145046° N, 122.9049755° W

Best Time to Visit: Spring to early fall when the park is lush and the waterfall is at its peak.

Pass/Permit/Fees: Entry to the park is free.

Did You Know? Tumwater Falls Park is home to a salmon hatchery, where you can witness salmon leaping up the falls during their spawning season.

Website: http://www.olytumfoundation.org/park.asp

VANCOUVER

Fort Vancouver National Historic Site

Step into history at the Fort Vancouver National Historic Site, a unique journey into the past of the Pacific Northwest. Located in the heart of Vancouver, this site offers visitors the opportunity to explore the reconstructed 19th century fur trading post and discover the stories of those who lived and worked there.

Location: 612 E Reserve St, Vancouver, WA 98661-3811

Closest City or Town: Vancouver, Washington

How to Get There: From I-5 take the Mill Plain Boulevard exit (Exit 1-C). Head East and follow signs to Fort Vancouver National Historic Site.

GPS Coordinates: 45.6257241° N, 122.6550397° W

Best Time to Visit: The site is open throughout the year, but spring and fall offer the most comfortable weather for outdoor exploring.

Pass/Permit/Fees: Entry fees apply, check the website for current prices.

Did You Know? The original Fort Vancouver was the largest European settlement in the Pacific Northwest.

Website: http://www.nps.gov/fova

Esther Short Park

Take a moment to relax and breathe in the refreshing green space of Esther Short Park, located in the heart of Vancouver. This vibrant urban park offers a children's playground, a rose garden, and a water feature for visitors to enjoy, creating an oasis within the bustling city.

Location: 605 Esther St, Vancouver, WA 98660-3021

Closest City or Town: Vancouver, Washington

How to Get There: From downtown Vancouver, head west on E Mill Plain Blvd toward E Reserve St, Turn right onto Esther St and you'll find the park on your left.

GPS Coordinates: 45.6261276° N, 122.675784° W

Best Time to Visit: Spring and summer when the roses are in bloom

Pass/Permit/Fees: Free admission

Did You Know? The park hosts the Vancouver Farmers Market every weekend from March until October.

Website: http://www.cityofvancouver.us/parksrec/page/esther-short-park

WALLA WALLA

Fort Walla Walla Museum

The Fort Walla Walla Museum in Walla Walla, Washington, can transport you back in time. The museum provides an in-depth history of the region, with displays of pioneers, military history, and indigenous cultures.

Location: 755 NE Myra Rd, Walla Walla, WA 99362-8035

Closest City or Town: Walla Walla, Washington

How to Get There: From downtown Walla Walla, take E Alder St and Wilbur Ave to Myra Rd in Walla Walla East, follow Myra Rd to the museum.

GPS Coordinates: 46.0475345° N, 118.3660067° W

Best Time to Visit: Open year-round, but spring and fall offer the most comfortable weather.

Pass/Permit/Fees: Admission fees apply. Please check the website for details.

Did You Know? Fort Walla Walla Museum is home to four exhibit halls, a pioneer village, and a 17-acre outdoor exhibit space.

Website: http://www.fwwm.org/

Whitman Mission

Step back in time and immerse yourself in history at the Whitman Mission, located in Walla Walla, WA. This mission site acts as a poignant reminder of the conflicts between settlers and indigenous tribes in the 19th century. Explore the well-preserved site, absorb the historical significance, and enjoy scenic views overlooking the beautiful Walla Walla Valley.

Location: 328 Whitman Mission Rd, Walla Walla, WA 99362

Closest City or Town: Walla Walla, Washington

How to Get There: From Walla Walla, head southwest on US-12 W. Take the exit for Whitman Mission Rd.

GPS Coordinates: 46.0413544° N, 118.4639745° W

Best Time to Visit: Open year-round, but the most pleasant weather can be enjoyed from late spring to early fall.

Pass/Permit/Fees: Free of charge.

Did You Know? Whitman Mission was the site of the infamous Whitman Massacre, a significant event in the history of the American West.

Website: http://www.nps.gov/whmi/

Mount St. Helens

Experience the raw power of nature at Mount St. Helens, an active stratovolcano located in Washington state's Cascade Range. The scenery dramatically changed after the 1980 eruption - the most catastrophic in U.S. history - creating a unique landscape that continues to evolve and recover.

Location: 24000 Spirit Lake Hwy, Toutle, WA 98649

Closest City or Town: Toutle, Washington

How to Get There: From I-5, take exit 49 and head east on Hwy 504 for 52 miles to reach the visitor center.

GPS Coordinates: 46.2752681° N, 122.2172109° W

Best Time to Visit: Spring to fall for hiking and viewing wildflowers

Pass/Permit/Fees: National Monument Pass required ($8/person)

Did You Know? The 1980 eruption reduced the elevation of the mountain's summit from 9,677 ft to 8,363 ft, replacing it with a 1-mile-wide crater.

Website: https://www.parks.wa.gov/245/Mount-St-Helens

Palouse Falls State Park

Journey to the heart of Washington's scenic beauty at Palouse Falls State Park. Marvel at the stunning waterfall cascading into a deep canyon, hike along the scenic trails and immerse yourself in the natural beauty of the park. The pull of nature is irresistible here!

Location: MQ7F+G3 La Crosse, Washington

Closest City or Town: La Crosse, Washington

How to Get There: From La Crosse, head west on Pine St toward S Star School Rd. Turn right at the 1st cross street onto S Star School Rd. The park will be on your left.

GPS Coordinates: 46.6638125° N, 118.2273125° W

Best Time to Visit: Spring and early summer when the falls are at their most powerful.

Pass/Permit/Fees: A Discover Pass is required for vehicle access to state parks for day use.

Did You Know? Palouse Falls was declared the official state waterfall of Washington in 2014!

Website: http://www.parks.wa.gov/559/Palouse-Falls

Ohme Gardens County Park

Experience nature's splendor at Ohme Gardens County Park, a beautiful oasis nestled in Wenatchee. Wander along stone pathways through the manicured gardens, soak in the panoramic views, and let the tranquility of the surrounding natural beauty captivate you.

Location: 3327 Ohme Rd, Wenatchee, WA 98801-9060

Closest City or Town: Wenatchee, Washington

How to Get There: From Wenatchee, head north on WA-285 N. Turn right onto Ohme Garden Rd.

GPS Coordinates: 47.4784935° N, 120.3270107° W

Best Time to Visit: The park is open from April through October, with peak blooms in the summer months.

Pass/Permit/Fees: Entrance fees apply. Please check the website for details.

Did You Know? Ohme Gardens has been a labor of love for the Ohme family, maintained and developed for over 90 years!

Website: http://www.ohmegardens.org/

Chateau Ste. Michelle Vineyards

Sip your way through Washington's oldest winery, Chateau Ste. Michelle Vineyards is nestled in the idyllic Sammamish River Valley. This historic estate offers a unique fusion of old-world charm and modern innovation, making it a must-visit destination for wine enthusiasts.

Location: 14111 NE 145th St, Woodinville, WA 98072-6981

Closest City or Town: Woodinville, Washington

How to Get There: From I-405 take exit 23 (SR 522) and go east. Take the first exit (SR 202) and turn right onto NE 145th St.

GPS Coordinates: 47.7290973° N, 122.1495743° W

Best Time to Visit: Spring and summer for outdoor concerts and wine events.

Pass/Permit/Fees: Wine tastings start at $15. Tours and experiences vary in price.

Did You Know? The Chateau was built in 1912 and is listed on the National Register of Historic Places.

Website: http://www.ste-michelle.com/?utm_source=tripadvisor&utm_medium=listing&utm_campaign=chateau+ste+michelle

MAP

We have devised an interactive map that includes all destinations described in the book.

Upon scanning a provided QR code, a link will be sent to your email, allowing you access to this unique digital feature.

This map is both detailed and user-friendly, marking every location described within the pages of the book. It provides accurate addresses and GPS coordinates for each location, coupled with direct links to the websites of these stunning destinations.

Once you receive your email link and access the interactive map, you'll have an immediate and comprehensive overview of each site's location. This invaluable tool simplifies trip planning and navigation, making it a crucial asset for both first-time visitors and seasoned explorers of Washington.

Scan the following QR or type in the provided link to receive it:

https://jo.my/wabucketlistform

You will receive an email with links to access the Interactive Map. If you do not see our email, please look for it in spam or another section of your inbox.

In case you have any problems, you can write us at
TravelBucketList@becrepress.com

Made in United States
North Haven, CT
07 April 2024